Praise for *Viral Churches*

"This book by . . . my dear friends and partners in ministry . . . is pure gold. . . . There is simply no better way to reach, teach, train, and send out disciples than through churches that are planted with the intentionality of planting others." —Rick Warren, Saddleback Church

"This book is for those who want to go from making a dent to making a difference." —Mark Driscoll, Mars Hill Church (www. marshillchurch.org), Acts 29 Network, The Resurgence

"There is no doubt that the idea of exponentially reproducing church is the next step, providing us with perhaps the only viable way forward to overcome the current impasse of Christianity in the West. In *Viral Churches*, Ed and Warren team up to produce a characteristically well researched, missiologically hefty, and definitive book for our times." —Alan Hirsch author, *The Forgotten Ways* and coauthor, *Untamed*

"Ed Stetzer's experience in planting churches and training pastors makes him one of today's most experienced and trusted voices. He has an ability to take research and make it applicable to this generation's Christian leaders. I applaud his efforts to build spiritual movements everywhere." —Steve Douglass, president, Campus Crusade for Christ International

Viral Churches

Helping Church Planters Become Movement Makers

Ed Stetzer and Warren Bird

A Leadership Network Publication

JOSSEY-BASS
A Wiley Imprint
www.josseybass.com

Published by Jossey-Bass

A Wiley Imprint

989 Market Street, San Francisco, CA 94103-1741—www.josseybass.com

Unless otherwise noted, all Scripture quotations are taken from the Holman Christian Standard Bible®, Copyright © 1999, 2000, 2002, 2003 by Holman Bible Publishers. Used by permission. Holman Christian Standard Bible®, Holman CSB®, and HCSB® are federally registered trademarks of Holman Bible Publishers.

Scripture quotations marked NLT are taken from the Holy Bible, New Living Translation, copyright 1996, 2004. Used by permission of Tyndale House Publishers, Inc., Wheaton, Illinois 60189. All rights reserved.

Scripture quotations from THE MESSAGE. Copyright © by Eugene H. Peterson 1993, 1994, 1995, 1996, 2000, 2001, 2002. Used by permission of NavPress Publishing Group.

Scripture quotations marked (NIV) are taken from the Holy Bible, New International Version®, NIV®. Copyright © 1973, 1978, 1984 by Biblica, Inc.™ Used by permission of Zondervan. All rights reserved worldwide.

Jossey-Bass books and products are available through most bookstores. To contact Jossey-Bass directly call our Customer Care Department within the U.S. at 800-956-7739, outside the U.S. at 317-572-3986, or fax 317-572-4002.

Jossey-Bass also publishes its books in a variety of electronic formats. Some content that appears in print may not be available in electronic books.

Library of Congress Cataloging-in-Publication Data

Stetzer, Ed.

   Viral churches : helping church planters become movement makers / Ed Stetzer and Warren Bird; foreword by Rick Warren — 1st ed.

      p. cm.

   Includes bibliographical references (p.) and index.

   ISBN 978-0-470-55045-8 (cloth)

1. Church development, New.   I. Bird, Warren.   II. Title.

   BV652.24.S73 2010

   254'.1097—dc22

                                                   2009048404

LEADERSHIP NETWORK TITLES

The Blogging Church: Sharing the Story of Your Church Through Blogs, Brian Bailey and Terry Storch

Church Turned Inside Out: A Guide for Designers, Refiners, and Re-Aligners, Linda Bergquist and Allan Karr

Leading from the Second Chair: Serving Your Church, Fulfilling Your Role, and Realizing Your Dreams, Mike Bonem and Roger Patterson

The Way of Jesus: A Journey of Freedom for Pilgrims and Wanderers, Jonathan S. Campbell with Jennifer Campbell

Leading the Team-Based Church: How Pastors and Church Staffs Can Grow Together into a Powerful Fellowship of Leaders, George Cladis

Organic Church: Growing Faith Where Life Happens, Neil Cole

Church 3.0: Upgrades for the Future of the Church, Neil Cole

Off-Road Disciplines: Spiritual Adventures of Missional Leaders, Earl Creps

Reverse Mentoring: How Young Leaders Can Transform the Church and Why We Should Let Them, Earl Creps

Building a Healthy Multi-Ethnic Church: Mandate, Commitments, and Practices of a Diverse Congregation, Mark DeYmaz

Leading Congregational Change Workbook, James H. Furr, Mike Bonem, and Jim Herrington

Baby Boomers and Beyond: Tapping the Ministry Talents and Passions of Adults over Fifty, Amy Hanson

The Tangible Kingdom: Creating Incarnational Community, Hugh Halter and Matt Smay

Leading Congregational Change: A Practical Guide for the Transformational Journey, Jim Herrington, Mike Bonem, and James H. Furr

The Leader's Journey: Accepting the Call to Personal and Congregational Transformation, Jim Herrington, Robert Creech, and Trisha Taylor

Whole Church: Leading from Fragmentation to Engagement, Mel Lawrenz

Culture Shift: Transforming Your Church from the Inside Out, Robert Lewis and Wayne Cordeiro, with Warren Bird

Church Unique: How Missional Leaders Cast Vision, Capture Culture, and Create Movement, Will Mancini

A New Kind of Christian: A Tale of Two Friends on a Spiritual Journey, Brian D. McLaren

The Story We Find Ourselves In: Further Adventures of a New Kind of Christian, Brian D. McLaren

Missional Renaissance: Changing the Scorecard for the Church, Reggie McNeal

Practicing Greatness: 7 Disciplines of Extraordinary Spiritual Leaders, Reggie McNeal

The Present Future: Six Tough Questions for the Church, Reggie McNeal

A Work of Heart: Understanding How God Shapes Spiritual Leaders, Reggie McNeal

The Millennium Matrix: Reclaiming the Past, Reframing the Future of the Church, M. Rex Miller

Shaped by God's Heart: The Passion and Practices of Missional Churches, Milfred Minatrea

The Missional Leader: Equipping Your Church to Reach a Changing World, Alan J. Roxburgh and Fred Romanuk

Missional Map-Making: Skills for Leading in Times of Transition, Alan J. Roxburgh

Relational Intelligence: How Leaders Can Expand Their Influence Through a New Way of Being Smart, Steve Saccone

Viral Churches: Helping Church Planters Become Movement Makers, Ed Stetzer and Warren Bird

The Externally Focused Quest: Becoming the Best Church for the Community, Eric Swanson and Rick Rusaw

The Ascent of a Leader: How Ordinary Relationships Develop Extraordinary Character and Influence, Bill Thrall, Bruce McNicol, and Ken McElrath

Beyond Megachurch Myths: What We Can Learn from America's Largest Churches, Scott Thumma and Dave Travis

The Elephant in the Boardroom: Speaking the Unspoken About Pastoral Transitions, Carolyn Weese and J. Russell Crabtree

CONTENTS

ABOUT LEADERSHIP NETWORK

Leadership Network, an initiative of OneHundredX, exists to honor God and serve others by investing in innovative church leaders who impact the Kingdom immeasurably.

Since 1984, Leadership Network has brought together exceptional leaders, who are focused on similar ministry initiatives, to accelerate their impact. The ensuing collaboration—often across denominational lines—provides a strong base from which individual leaders can better analyze and refine their individual strategies. Creating an environment for collaborative discovery, dialogue, and sharing encourages leaders to extend their own innovations and ideas. Leadership Network further enhances this process through the development and distribution of highly targeted ministry tools and resources—including video, podcasts, concept papers, special research reports, e-publications, and books like this one.

With Leadership Network's assistance, today's Christian leaders are energized, equipped, inspired—and better able to multiply their own dynamic Kingdom-building initiatives.

In 1996 Leadership Network partnered with Jossey-Bass, a Wiley imprint, to develop a series of creative books that would provide thought leadership to innovators in church ministry. Leadership Network Publications present thoroughly researched and innovative concepts from leading thinkers, practitioners, and pioneering churches. The series collectively draws from a wide range of disciplines, with individual titles providing perspective on one or more of five primary areas:

- Enabling effective leadership
- Encouraging life-changing service
- Building authentic community
- Creating Kingdom-centered impact
- Engaging cultural and demographic realities

For additional information on the mission or activities of Leadership Network activities, please contact:

Leadership Network
2626 Cole Avenue,
Suite 900
Dallas, Texas 75204
800.765.5323
www.leadnet.org
client.care@leadnet.org

FOREWORD BY RICK WARREN

The single most effective method for fulfilling the Great Commission that Jesus gave us is to plant new churches! Two thousand years of Christian history have proven that new churches grow faster, and reach more people, than established churches. The growth on any plant is always on the newest branches.

This is why this book by Ed Stetzer and Warren Bird, my dear friends and longtime partners in ministry, is so vitally important. *Vital Churches* casts a clear and compelling vision that calls for every local congregation, regardless of size or age, to make church multiplication a fundamental component of their evangelism strategy.

There is simply no better way to reach, teach, train, and send disciples out into the world than through churches that are planted with the intention of planting others. And for churches, or denominations, that have plateaued or are declining, church planting is an indispensible ingredient for renewal and revitalization. It is the fastest way to infuse new life and new people into atrophied fellowships.

No single congregation can possibly reach every type of person in its community. It takes new churches to reach new generations and new groups of people. And, as I first stated in 1980 when I planted Saddleback, "It's far easier to have babies than to raise the dead!"

It is also more fun.

My friends, Ed and Warren, make it clear that church multiplication is not some new-fangled strategy of the twenty-first century. It is our oldest strategy—a return to the way the first century church did evangelism, by starting new congregations everywhere the Good News was shared. This is why "Plant Churches" is the first letter of our network's global P.E.A.C.E. strategy.

All pastors want their churches to grow up, not just grow larger. We want to see a mature, healthy church that balances all five of God's purposes given to us in the Great Commandment and Great Commission: Worship ("Love God with all your heart"), Ministry ("Love your neighbor as yourself"), Evangelism ("Go and make disciples"), Edification ("Teach them *to do* everything I've commanded you"), and Fellowship ("Baptize them" into the Body of Christ).

But how do you know when a church is spiritually mature? When it begins to reproduce itself! Physical maturity (after puberty) is evidenced by the ability to have babies. In the same way, a church is not spiritually mature until it starts having spiritual babies—reproducing new churches.

There really is no excuse for not planting churches. Your church doesn't have to be large, wealthy, or established to plant a church.

When I planted Saddleback Church, we made a commitment to plant at least one new church a year, so at the end of our first year, when our attendance was around 130, we planted our first daughter church. We've started as least one new church a year for the past thirty years, and have started as many as seventeen in a single year out of our church.

You'd be surprised at how effective new believers and fledgling members can be at church planting. I recently met with the original small group of people who helped me plant Saddleback thirty years ago.

Most of them were saved at Saddleback during the first year. I asked them "How many of you ever thought you could be a church planter when we began Saddleback?" Not one of them raised their hand. Then I asked, "How many of you would say today that starting Saddleback Church is the greatest thing you've ever done with your life?" Every single one of them raised their hand! The congregation we planted will outlast all of us.

As a pastor who has personally supervised the planting of hundreds of churches, and having trained tens of thousands of church planters across 162 countries over the past thirty years, I know what works and what doesn't work when it comes to church multiplication. So believe me when I tell you that this book by my partners is pure gold.

I invite you to join us in the grand adventure!

Dr. Rick Warren
Saddleback Church
P.E.A.C.E. Coalition
Twitter @RickWarren

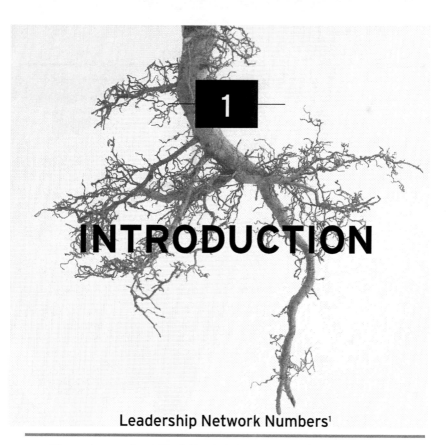

INTRODUCTION

Leadership Network Numbers[1]

- **It's no longer true that the total number of churches is declining**

   An important shift happened in recent years. After decades of net decline, more U.S. churches are being started each year (approximately 4,000) than are being closed each year (approximately 3,500).[2]

- **The greatest increase of new churches is on the "network" level**

   There is a growing involvement in churches planting churches and a moderately growing involvement in denominations planting churches, but the greatest motion is through networks planting churches, which are increasing at a *rapid* level.[3]

Do you see anything unusual in the following vision statement taken from a new church's Web site?

OUR VISION

Imagine Fellowship* plans to reach and grow thousands for Christ in San Antonio, Texas. Imagine Fellowship will also train a new generation of leaders who have the heart and drive to start churches over the entire United States. We will plant a church in every city that has 100,000 or more (there are roughly 262 cities). These churches will also train church planters so that every city has a church that is engaging the next generation for Christ.

Scripture
God can do anything—you know, far more than you could ever imagine or guess or request in your wildest dreams! (Ephesians 3:20, The Message)

Ten years ago, you would have had to look far and wide to find a church with such vision. Today churches like Imagine Fellowship with a vision for multiplication are springing up everywhere; so many, in fact, that we were inspired to write this book. We believe that we are on the edge of seeing an exponential multiplication movement in the United States, and that these churches are leading the way.

What's so different about Imagine Fellowship's vision?

1. The church wants to plant other churches, but not just one or two or even five or ten. They've set their sights on *more than two hundred of them!*

2. The church is up front about this vision from day one. Other churches tend to wait for some feeling of stability or

---

*All churches and church networks named in this book are listed in the Appendix, including their Web sites. Our reference to a diversity of churches and denominations doesn't mean we endorse all of their beliefs and practices.

preparedness before they consider planting other churches. Imagine Fellowship is different—they're not waiting to become well established before thinking about multiplication. Instead they're building it into their DNA. In fact, Imagine's vision statement has more words in it about replication than on the initial ministry in San Antonio!

3. The "owner" of the vision is the local church. This isn't just the pastor's new missions campaign, and it's not something being handed down from a denomination or adopted from a network. This call to multiplication is a churchwide thing, and today it's local churches like this that are setting the pace for their denominations or associations.

4. Imagine went to work on this initiative immediately. It held its first meeting as a new church in November 2008 and within months began training its first church planter. It has taken on two more since that time.

5. The church has been influenced by its relationship with another church, one with a similar vision of reaching those who do not know Christ. In this case, Imagine Fellowship's Pastor Kevin Joyce previously served on staff with what they call their "parent church"—Bay Area Fellowship in Corpus Christi, Texas. As the "About Us" section of their Web site says, "Pastor Kevin worked under Pastor Bil Cornelius for two years and is now going to bring a unique experience to San Antonio, Texas."

Church planting is good. A vision for a church multiplication movement is better.

Many of you will not be content with a one-off church plant that serves only to replace a dying church. You share Imagine Fellowship's vision for massive church multiplication. *Viral Churches* is our effort to fan that flame of your passion and give you some new insights as to how it can be accomplished.

National Awakening

Imagine Fellowship is not alone. We know this because of a huge research project commissioned by Leadership Network (where Warren directs the research division), conducted by Ed Stetzer and LifeWay Research (which Ed leads). The data collection and analysis took place in 2007 with relevant information updated in the fall of 2009 for this book. This was arguably the most comprehensive study ever done to review the methods, trends, and outcomes of church planting organizations across the United States. It involved a team of twenty-one people who contacted, surveyed, summarized, and evaluated leaders including

The Leadership Network research project was arguably the most comprehensive study ever done to review the methods, trends, and outcomes of church planting organizations across the United States.

- 200-plus church planting churches
- 100-plus leaders from forty denominations
- 45 church planting networks
- 84 organic church leaders
- 12 nationally known experts
- 53 colleges and seminaries
- 54 doctoral dissertations
- 41 journal articles
- 100-plus church planting books and manuals

The original findings were condensed into four free "State of Church Planting USA" reports at Leadership Network's Web site, www.leadnet.org/churchplantingresources. Report titles are

- *Church Planting Overview*
- *Funding New Churches*

- *Improving the Health and Survivability of New Churches*
- *Who Starts New Churches*

This book takes findings from the original project and reframes it to inform, guide, and even catalyze today's many church planting leaders, especially those heading, forming, or considering a church planting network. Our hope is to inspire and help you develop a church multiplication movement—an exponential birth of new churches that engage lost people and that replicate themselves through even more new churches. A church multiplication movement is a rapid reproduction of churches planting churches, measured by a reproduction rate of 50 percent through the third generation of churches, with new churches having 50 percent new converts. To achieve such momentum, churches would need to plant, on average, a new church every two years with each church reaching at least half of its attendees from the unchurched community. We believe this rapid reproduction of churches needs to happen among hundreds of niche population groups—from SUV-driving young families in fast-growing suburbs to urban hipster environmentalists to unchurched rural country music lovers.

> *Our hope is to inspire and help you develop a church multiplication movement—an exponential birth of new churches that engage lost people and that replicate themselves through even more new churches—measured by a reproduction rate of 50 percent through the third generation of churches, with new churches having 50 percent new converts.*

These days it seems that many people are talking about church planting movements, but we want to move beyond theory to actual doing. This book is to be a practical guide for orchestrating a movement. It will address the idea of what to do next in your church planting strategies, in light of research on what's actually working best and within a context of kingdom-minded, Scripture-based theology.

We're not just going to describe those church planting movements that we believe God has sparked in certain parts of the world. We're prescribing them as the much-needed alternative to inward-focused or addition-based church planting. Though this book is research based, we also take an advocacy perspective. *Viral Churches* will contain enough stories for participants in church planting at every level to find inspiration and specific help. But most of all, it will speak to a new breed of people who want to populate this country (and beyond), saturating it with a viral movement of multiplying churches.

A virus doesn't re-create itself from scratch. Instead, it infects existing cells to spread a disease. Viral marketing leverages existing social networks to spread ideas. In the same way, we believe that the kingdom of God can spread virally by "infecting" every tribe, group, club, neighborhood, community, and family. For that to happen, more people have to shift from church planting to church multiplication movements. If we were writing to an audience that loves math, we could have titled the book *Multiply Everything: From Church Planting to Movement Making*. Or perhaps *New Math Church: You Can Move from Planting to Multiplying Churches*. But it's not just math; it's relational as well, hence the term *Viral*.

According to the research, a church multiplication movement could happen, but it hasn't yet. We want to show you what the pioneers are learning, cheer the amazing things God is doing through them, encourage you to become one of the pioneers, and show how you too can be part of a multiplication movement.

Who Needs to Know

We think everyone ought to care about church planting and we're a little surprised when they don't. The church is called the Bride of Christ (among other great names), and who wouldn't want the bride to flourish? However, too many Christians love Jesus but not his church and its mission. We're naive enough to believe that you can't love Jesus and neglect his wife.

Thus our primary audience is people who love the church and care especially about its multiplication, particularly leaders involved in church planting across the English-speaking world. If you consider yourself a church planter (or would like to), this book is for you. Whether your endeavor started intentionally or spontaneously, this book is for you. If you're the head of an agency, coalition, parachurch organization, partnership or denomination, this book is for you. Whether you're bi-vocational, fully funded, or unfunded, this book is for you. If you're a seminary professor, Bible student, pastoral intern, volunteer, professional, or an innocent bystander, this book is for you.

Some of you are church planters who have seen multiple plants spring up through your leadership. Maybe you're planting a church but have a desire for multiple plants to follow through your leadership. Some of you could lead networks and movements of new churches—you just don't

> *Some of you could lead networks and movements of new churches— you just don't know it yet.*

know it yet. Some of you *will* lead the next movements of new churches. When you see the big picture of what God is doing, we believe your vision will expand for how your church can be part of a replicating movement.

Some of you are just exploring the idea of multiplication. If you've figured out that multiplying is better than adding, and if you're intrigued by what happens when you birth multiple churches, all of which in turn plant other churches, this book is for you.

You may be surprised to learn that you are not alone. Many people who are initiating networks have not yet met or heard of each other. We hope you will be encouraged to read the stories and strategies of others. Each chapter will introduce you to at least one network, coalition, or denomination that is placing a major emphasis on church planting, and the Appendix lists all the entities that have been described.

Although most examples are from North America, you do not have to live here to apply the ideas of this book. You might be a church planter or missionary in another country. Some countries beyond North America are way ahead of us, as we discuss later, but we can all learn from what God is doing among us.

Our prayer is that many more followers of Jesus in the next generation will become church planters. We recall the command of Jesus: "The harvest is abundant, but the workers are few. Therefore, pray to the Lord of the harvest to send out workers into His harvest" (Matthew 9:37–38).

Our Approach

Each chapter begins with a research finding called "Leadership Network Numbers," mostly taken from our major research project. The chapter itself then focuses on a related practical idea that we believe is essential to the success of church multiplication networks. Together the chapters all suggest both a perspective and strategy for the day when "churches planting churches that in turn plant churches" becomes as common and normal as churches with multiple services or churches that send service teams after disasters such as the 2004 Indian Ocean tsunami or Hurricane Katrina in 2005.

Each chapter makes a different point:

- Church planting is the new evangelism (Chapter Two)
- Church planting may be mainstream, but church multiplication is not (Chapter Three)
- Aggressive local churches and church planting networks are leading the way where denominations once did (Chapter Four)

- Church planters are cooperating by learning together at unprecedented levels (Chapter Five)
- The way church planters are recruited, assessed, and deployed offer strong predictors of their success (Chapter Six)
- New church survivability has increased dramatically (Chapter Seven)
- House churches evangelize and replicate effectively—sometimes! (Chapter Eight)
- Multisite strategy is a growing trend among reproducing churches (Chapter Nine)
- Some churches grow fast, but that's not the same as reproduction (Chapter Ten)
- In funding new churches, partnerships matter (Chapter Eleven)
- Missional replication still faces several obstacles (Chapter Twelve)
- A church multiplication movement requires a new scorecard (Chapter Thirteen)
- Several serious challenges still lay ahead (Chapter Fourteen)

You can read the material in any order, so feel free to start with whatever chapter intrigues you most. There is, however, a sense of flow. Step by step, we advocate what has happened and what still must happen for a true church multiplication movement to be birthed.

Wherever you begin, our hope is that each chapter will give you new information (or confirmation of what you had already experienced). But we also want to lead you to a greater vision and dream of what God has begun to do, and might do even more powerfully as you connect the dots for your potential role.

The Authors

Church planters are a cocky lot. They don't want to read books on church planting from armchair experts who met a church planter once. So, to establish our legitimacy, we need to tell you about our church planting background.

Although we are both now involved in full-time church research, we are also pastors who have led church plants, studied church plants and coached church planters. Each of us has three or more academic degrees in theology plus a research-based doctorate (Warren is impressed that Ed has *two* earned doctorates!). We've both authored or coauthored a number of books. Web sites with more details about us, including contact information, are listed at the end of the book (see pages 12–15 and 233–235). You will also find out that neither of us is shy about sharing our thoughts on all things church, doctrine, and the Gospel.

Most of all, we're both passionate that the United States is a receptive mission field and we believe that God could use this very generation to change both the face and the fruitfulness of today's church—but only if certain changes happen.

To find out the good things that are happening, and what we hope is ahead in the world of church planting, please turn the page.

Ed Stetzer
Nashville, TN

Warren Bird
Suffern, NY

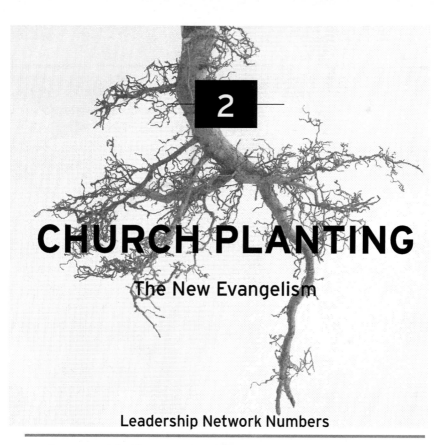

CHURCH PLANTING

The New Evangelism

Leadership Network Numbers

- **Some Models Yield Higher Conversions Than Others**

Our research indicates that the current best practices, in terms of producing more evangelistic conversions, are seeker approaches, purpose-driven approaches, and ethnic church planting.[1]

- **Churches Among Ethnic Groups Find Strong Responsiveness**

The noticeable increase in ethnic church planting is most obvious among immigrants. The largest recent groups of newcomers to this country, according to the U.S. Census Bureau, are (in order) from Mexico, China, Philippines, India, El Salvador, Vietnam, Korea, and Cuba.[2]

We are writing this book because we are absolutely convinced that a huge influx of new churches is required in this country, an influx that will not happen unless present patterns change. We believe church planting is the best way to take the church to the people it needs to serve. We believe new churches are the best platform for followers of Jesus to live as salt, light, and doers of good deeds in our communities (Matthew 5: 13–16), to demonstrate love in practical ways (Matthew 22:34–40; John 13:35), and to intentionally make more disciples of Jesus Christ (Matthew 28:19–20).

We are encouraged by the recently increased interest in church planting. It's unfortunate, though, that the trend focuses largely on addition rather than multiplication. We want to lay the foundation for an out-of-control replication of new churches, a movement of God that will literally change the landscape of North America.

This book is about laying the foundation for an out-of-control replication of new churches, a movement of God that will literally change the landscape of North America.

It will not be neat. It will not be orderly. But when spontaneous movements authored by God occur, there is a tendency to shake up the status quo. We think it can't happen soon enough!

If such a movement happens, many more people will find peace with God, purpose in life, and an eternal destiny in heaven. This is the sort of kingdom work that we as Christians need to be about.

We Confess: We Began with Addition

If only we had known then what we know now. The vision we inherited was shortsightedly fixed on addition. For both of us, our initial assignment as a "pastor" was to start a new church in a community that needed Jesus. We did plant churches but they weren't intentional about building multiplication into their DNA. In the grand scheme of things, all we did was to add some new churches. Each replicated a precious community of faith but few have replicated themselves, much less multiplied themselves.

Ed planted his first church even before going to seminary. He was twenty-one years old and started a church among the urban poor in Buffalo, New York. He had no seminary training or previous pastoral experience. The home mission board of his denomination turned him down as a church planter. Yet he was convinced that this was what God wanted him to do, so with his wife, Donna, he followed God's leadership and went forward. It took them on a journey that was really difficult, spiritually dangerous, and financially irresponsible. But, above all of those things, it was absolutely worth the price they paid.

Though Buffalo was the fastest-shrinking city in America at the time, Ed and Donna witnessed God's Spirit poured out into their new neighborhood. They learned that evangelism can be done anywhere there are people. Contrary to popular practice, not every church plant has to take place among upper-middle class white people in a rapidly growing suburb of a metropolitan city. In fact, while planting in downtown Buffalo, Ed learned that God desired to multiply the effect of his kingdom in a place many thought implausible. Working a full-time job (blowing insulation) Ed devoted his evenings and weekend to planting a church.

Ed and Donna moved into the neighborhood with nothing but the Gospel, a passion for people to hear it, and a willingness to abandon all previous methods to make it a reality. Soon enough, God began to multiply their efforts. Ed honestly doesn't know if an established church could have connected with the kind of people they did. In fact, churches already in that urban center were largely ineffective at making those connections.

Looking through the eyes of the urban poor of Buffalo, they saw afresh that planting a church is often the most effective way to reach someone for Christ. Why? Because a church plant does not know it has any limit on what it can do for God's kingdom. It is free from the baggage of past traditions, practices, and the "we've never done that before" mentality that plagues churches that have been around for awhile. From one church plant, exponential kingdom growth can occur—if the leader will point the people in that direction.

Before Warren became a church planter, he worked his way through seminary by writing a "Growing Church" column in his denomination's magazine. In it he profiled churches that were doing bold and creative things to help people find new life in Jesus Christ. Sometimes district superintendents suggested churches for him to interview. Sometimes he'd analyze annual reports to find an angle for a column, such as "the church with the highest percentage of adult conversions." One day it suddenly dawned on him that from both approaches, the majority of the churches with the most exciting cases of new life in Christ tended to be newly started ones. Or they were the rare established church that was busy starting other churches. It was an "aha" moment for Warren. He remembers reasoning, "When I graduate, if I want to make the greatest difference in bringing people to faith in Jesus Christ, I should probably plant a church." He and his wife, Michelle, started praying together about it.

Warren remembers reading C. Peter Wagner's oft-quoted statement that "the single most effective evangelistic methodology under heaven is planting new churches."[3] That certainly matched what he had discussed in the columns he wrote and what he had experienced in his childhood as part of a new church. His denomination, also realizing the harvest potential of new churches, wanted to launch many more new churches. They gave Warren and Michelle a green light and some start-up funds—and promised to follow up with a monthly phone call to ask how it was going.

Immediately upon graduation, Warren started a church in a community that had not encountered a new church in over a hundred years—but did have dozens of new synagogues and mosques (which should have told him something!). Warren recruited a core group of five adults, which was far too small, but all of them were naive and full of faith.

God honored their passion. Half of their attendees became new believers. Many of them are still their good friends. One remains a weekly prayer partner with Michelle to this day. All five members of their core group went on to become church planting missionaries and life-long friends. In fact they recently visited one of these friends in Asia.

Life as a church planter was often hard, mostly because of immature decisions Warren made, but they wouldn't trade that chapter in their lives for anything. Nor would their children—who are all young adults today, living in other cities and each involved as volunteers in a church plant! Warren and Michelle, after their first church planting experience, were subsequently involved in two other church plants.

Warren, his wife, and their children are all drawn to church planting because it takes them to the front lines of ministry. They know that North America is one of the largest mission fields in the world today, and they see new churches as having great potential for reaching the unreached.

Both of us have experienced outreach efforts in new church plants and in older churches. Frankly, there is a difference. It is not necessarily a difference in the methods. It is a difference of ethos held by those who are a part of a new church and their struggle to "overwhelm" a community with the Gospel's power. In these environments, evangelism simply overpowers the need for self-preserving ministries that tend to use up the energies of the core once a church becomes established.

We Suspect You're Smarter Than We Were

There are a lot of "Eds" and "Warrens" out there who are likewise embarking on their inaugural mission as church planters. Maybe you're smart enough to have realized that planting one church is not enough. We hope it will help you to learn from our experiences and from leading practitioners around the country.

If you're a new church planter, you might be interested to know that we've each written other books for first-time church planters, offering specific nuts and bolts about actual church planting. You'll find these titles in The Authors later in this book; others we recommend are listed in the Bibliography.

However, please keep reading this book as well! Here you will find a dramatically expanded vision for what it means not just to start one church, or even to be a replicating church, but to be part of what may become a movement of multiplying church plants.

In short, this is not a book for those whose approach is to start only *one* church. Instead, we're speaking to those who have a dream of starting *lots and lots* of churches. Not via one-by-one addition, but by multiplication.

We want to help people like you go to new levels. And for those with a vision for multiplication, we want to introduce you to others who are perhaps like you. By showing you what others are doing, we hope to give you inspiration and specific ideas to see an even greater movement happen through your own church.

> *"The single most effective evangelistic methodology under heaven is planting new churches"* who in turn reproduce themselves.
>
> —C. PETER WAGNER

We even want to suggest a modification to the C. Peter Wagner quote (with our change in italics): "the single most effective evangelistic methodology under heaven is planting new churches" *who in turn reproduce themselves.*

Here's our logic. Does the following progression make sense to you?

- Recent years have seen an aggressive increase in the number of new churches being launched across the United States.

- In fact, church planting is on the mind of North American Christians at unprecedented levels. Not since the pioneer days of settling the west has this country seen such an emphasis on church planting.

- The current pace of roughly four thousand new churches being started every year now exceeds the number of churches being closed each year.[4]

> *Not since the pioneer days of settling the west has this country seen such an emphasis on church planting.*

- There are now more books, conferences and other resources available to church planters than have ever existed. Ed and Warren both know this firsthand—both have written books, Ed regularly speaks at many of the conferences, and Warren has helped convene numerous leadership community groups of church planters through Leadership Network.

Where do all these developments lead? With so many church planters out there, certain tipping points are being reached. As we progress through the rest of this book, we will point out a number of the changes that a planter must make to become the leader of a movement. For those leading movements, we hope that they will serve as catalysts to spur your vision even further. For those who may resist movemental expansion of new churches, we're hoping to raise up your replacements!

Combining all these concepts together, we find there's a new sort of person who is taking the lead in these very exciting developments. This person has a vision

> *Combining all these concepts together, we find there's a new person who is taking the lead in these very exciting developments.*

The keystone of their vision is the multiplication of people who trust personally in Christ as the Savior.

greater than just to plant one church: a vision not limited to starting a handful of churches either. Rather, their God-given passion is to develop an entire *network* of churches, all of whom have a vision to keep reproducing. And the keystone of the vision is the multiplication of churches for a reason: the multiplication of people who trust personally in Christ as the Savior.

Some call that leader "apostolic." We're OK with that term as long as we are describing the role of an initiator who plants churches that in turn plant more churches. As Ed wrote in *Breaking the Missional Code*:

> The meaning of the word *apostolic* is best defined as one who is "authoritatively sent." We are sent to proclaim the Gospel from Christ, who, before giving the Great Commission, began by reminding his listeners, "All authority in heaven and on earth has been give to me. Therefore go. . . ." (Matthew 28:18–19, NIV). Jesus authoritatively sends us to proclaim the Gospel and reach people in the name of Christ, not to lord it over in new structures of church life. Some claiming to be "apostolic" focus on their authority, but our focus is on Christ's authoritative commands to go and transform the world for the Gospel—in our church, community, and culture. . . . To be a biblical church means to be missionally engaged.[5]

The person with apostolic gifting doesn't just want to plant an individual church and be its pastor. That person wants to plant a *movement*.

Consider two congregations, Church A and Church Z.

Church A starts one church a year for the next twenty years. That's terrific. That's far beyond what most churches do in a lifetime. If that happened, a lot of lost people would be found and a lot of broken lives would be restored and transformed. We're totally in favor of Church A.

Most books on church planting are written to support and develop a church like that. If church planting were likened to horticulture, Church A is trying to plant one healthy tree a year.

But the Church Z people we're describing see things differently. They see an open fertile field and they don't want to plant one tree at a time. They want to fill the entire field with healthy orchards. This means they're thinking about new levels of fertilizing, watering, pruning and pollinating. They're even thinking about the different types of "trees" that should be planted. They like to ponder the age-old question, "How many future apple trees are in this one apple?"

To use the *Viral Churches* metaphor, they want to infect the world with a life-changing "malady," one that changes them and makes them carriers of the good news of Jesus. In church language, these Church Z leaders are adding missiological perspectives to sociological understanding of the community in order to increase their disciple-making impact. Those who lead or work with Church Z want to reproduce dozens of churches. They have an interest in church networks and church multiplication movements.

Church multiplication movement leaders work under a more intense impulse than other church planters. While others are fulfilling God's current agenda, these leaders seem to sense undercurrents of the next movement of God. We think that apostolic leadership does not have anything to do with a title (or liturgical attire in some cases) but rather God is raising up some who are anointed with a leadership gift, ability to teach and passion for multiplication.

We're writing this book primarily to serve the people who work with Church Z—or would like to help Church A *become* a Church Z. This book speaks most directly to those who dream of seeing today's many streams of church planting come together conceptually into a river of unified movement, the kind marked by replication and multiplication.

In short, we're writing to people whose basic goal is not just to see a new church planted, but multiple churches planting multiple new churches, which in turn plant multiple new churches. This is the basis of not just a network, but a movement.

Evangelism Model from the Book of Acts?

Today there are a lot of books out there on church planting. That's good (well, *most* of them are good). But we also need to look at the Bible itself. Planting a church without looking to the New Testament is like becoming a congressional representative in Washington, D.C. without ever reading what the U.S. Constitution says. So we think we have to go back to *the* book and look at how the whole New Testament is saturated with the idea of church planting, especially the book of Acts, where we swim in it.

Multiplicative church planting is evangelism. This isn't the latest trend, theory, or program. Church planting is the dominant method of evangelism in the book of Acts, and the key to spreading the Gospel to every people group or population segment, large or small, in every corner of the planet. The term *people group*, used by anthropologists and missiologists, is an ethnolinguistic group of people—those who speak a common language and share a common culture. Examples include Cherokee Native Americans (a small population) and English-speaking Americans (a large population that includes Ed and Warren). A *population segment* would be more narrowly focused, such as taxi drivers in New York City.

The early church was a miracle of "spontaneous expansion." The world saw a rapid multiplication of churches across the Roman Empire and beyond. The clear strategy of the early church, starting with the commission from Jesus in Acts 1:8, is that followers of Jesus will not keep the Gospel for themselves, but will reproduce it over and over again in others. This led to churches that birthed other churches—and sent out leaders (whom we call missionaries) to start even more churches.

For years, most Bible teachers have referred to Paul's travels as his "missionary journeys." We prefer to call them Paul's "church planting journeys." Maybe we should

Most Bible teachers have referred to Paul's travels as his "missionary journeys." We prefer to call them Paul's "church planting journeys."

also call them a model for us, as Paul says "imitate me"—but let's just pretend at this point that only special people go on missionary or church planting *journeys*.

Throughout the book of Acts, we see the Christians constantly harassed and scattered. Without knowing it or meaning to, the religious and political authorities were helping believers become church planting missionaries. Everywhere the Christians went, they established a new gathering for worship, study, and ministry. When persecution broke out against the church in Jerusalem, believers "were scattered throughout the land of Judea and Samaria" (Acts 8:1)—and they took the Gospel with them.

Philip was an early church leader who went into Samaria. The response was so overwhelming that Peter and John joined him in the work (Acts 8:14) and went throughout Samaria to spread the Gospel (8:25). This is one of the places where we see the spontaneous building up of the church and gatherings beginning in multiple places due to God's work through a few leaders.

Acts 11:19–26 records another great movement of the Gospel. In this passage, the scattered believers move throughout Phoenicia, Cyprus, and Antioch. As a result, new churches are established. The church in Antioch becomes the new "headquarters" for the church. It is even in this city that Barnabas brings the conspicuous Saul to live and learn with the new church for a year (verses 25–26). Imagine the impact it had on Saul to see the spontaneous movements of the Spirit in establishing new churches in these regions!

Later, after Saul's name is changed to Paul, he and Barnabas preached in Pisidian Antioch and see many of the Gentiles rejoice at hearing the Gospel. But trouble is stirred up by the "religious women of high standing and the leading men of the city" (13:50). (Don't they sound like a fun bunch of people?) So what do the adventurous Paul and Barnabas do? Head to a new city to plant the Gospel there as well!

Throughout, the book of Acts cites stories of the Gospel being planted in city after city. In Thessalonica, Jason opens his house for a new expression of the church (17:7). Titius Justus and Crispis become leaders of a new church in Corinth (18:8–9). Later in the same chapter, Priscilla and Aquilla are left in Ephesus to establish a new work (verses 18–19). Even the young Timothy is sent with Erastus to Macedonia to plant a church in that region (19:21–22).

The application: in order for the Gospel to go somewhere, a messenger had to carry it. And wherever messengers went with it, we see churches established. Thus, we have the many letters of the New Testament written not to believers in Corinth, Ephesus, or Thessalonica but to *churches* gathered in those places.

The character central to all of these stories was Paul. He was always either going somewhere or sending others to go. Christians have often painted him as the champion of evangelism, master of open-air preaching, and an expert in apologetics. But, at the core of his ministry in the ancient world was the planting of a copious amount of churches. In Romans 15:20–21, God gives us an insight into Paul's character and how it happened through his life. It says:

> *Paul planted new churches that in turn planted new churches.*

"So my aim is to evangelize where Christ has not been named, in order that I will not be building on someone else's foundation, but, as it is written: Those who had no report of Him will see, and those who have not heard will understand."

Paul's heart was to see God glorified through the saving of the lost. But he lacked interest in "backing up" another ministry.

He wanted to forge new evangelistic territory for Christ by establishing new places where people gathered to worship and proclaim God's message. Paul's evangelistic strategy was to plant new churches that in turn planted new churches.

Today's Commission: Go and Plant Churches of All People

Maybe Ed and Warren are biased. Like irritated Mac users, they have had an experience and now think everyone should be free of the evil bondages of the PC and be born again to a Mac. They're planters and they think planting is a big deal.

But it's not just them. An intriguing article in *Christianity Today* talked about the most effective kinds of evangelism in recent decades.[6] The report started with the peak era for evangelistic crusades (such as Billy Graham, tent revivals, and so on) and worked forward to recent years. Fifty years ago, if church members wanted to do a better job of sharing the Gospel with their neighbors, they invited an evangelist to come to town. "If we get people to come," the thinking was, "the preacher will get them saved." As fewer and fewer churches used such approaches, people found new angles, such as bus ministry or the personal sharing of Gospel tracts.

Over time additional approaches emerged that seemed to work better for people to share the good news about Jesus with their families, friends, and neighbors. Christian movies, from 1992's *A Thief in the Night* to 2008's *Fireproof*, were designed to communicate the Gospel into popular culture. Mimicking mainstream successes in the 1980s and 1990s, Christian rock music made inroads into secular markets despite having Christian lyrics. Many ministries produce materials that help believers find elements of gospel truth in Hollywood films, on television and in best-selling books. No matter the era of history, the church has constantly searched for the most effective method of evangelizing their community.

Through it all, planting new churches has come in and out of favor with established churches.

The landing point for current times? "Today church planting is the default mode for evangelism," *Christianity Today* concludes.

"Today church planting is the default mode for evangelism," Christianity Today *concludes.*

Most denominations, when asked what they are doing to grow, "will refer you to their church planting office," it explains.

This is quite a shift from past decades. Ed remembers well the response of his friends when he felt called to plant his first church. They asked, "Could you not get a real church?" Fair enough—and he soon found out why. Many of the other people planting churches in the area told him that they were planting because they could not get a good church job—so they got on the denominational dole and tried to plant for a few years. Church planting was odd then, but now it is a mainstream form of outreach—and not just a place to gather up Christians.

In decades past, church planting was often more about transfer growth. Denominations often started a new church to service "their" people who had moved to gentrified downtowns or growing suburbs. The first time Ed ever taught church planting was with a legendary missions professor named Cal Guy. Cal explained that the way they planted churches back in the 1950s involved "chasing license plates." He explained that his church planters (primarily southerners) would plant churches in a town like Chicago by finding other displaced southerners. It really wasn't that hard. They'd start by finding the one grocery story in town that sold grits. When someone bought grits (or had a license plate from a southern state) they would get an invitation to the new church. Such "planting" was really "starting" because few unbelievers were reached. It was largely putting sheep in new pens.

Today the clear emphasis of most church planting is on evangelism, which the fruit confirms. The Southern Baptist Convention is not only the nation's largest Protestant denomination but also the denomination that plants more churches annually than any other group. Among *established* Southern Baptist churches, for example, there are 3.4 baptisms per one hundred resident members, but their *new* churches average 11.7. That's more than three times more! Other denominations offer similar numbers. It's not hard to conclude that the launching of more new churches will lead more people to Christ.

New churches today tend to remain focused outward and in tune with their communities, which helps explain their higher ratio of conversions and baptisms. They also have the advantage of being at the front end of their life cycle, not yet struggling with mission drift.

Mission drift occurs as a church is established and new ministries are formed that serve the needs within the congregation. There is nothing inherently wrong with children's choirs, Saturday men's breakfasts, or student lock-ins, though student lock-ins are from the pit—but that is for another book. These ministries may be effective but they are often inwardly focused; they are more about keeping churched people comfortable than about reaching out.

Our point is that typical church programming often steals energy and time from the original mission focus of the church, which is to see lives changed through the Gospel. New churches typically have fewer programs and therefore less to distract them from the main thing. They remain solidly tied to the mission.

Unfortunately, many churches have not only experienced mission drift but have redefined their mission according to where they have drifted. We know we've drifted when church planting becomes about expanding an earthly kingdom or making church more comfortable and convenient for believers. When church planting turns into a turf war with existing churches, we've drifted. When churches are planted out of reaction to methodologies rather than in response to the Great Commission, we've drifted. When church planting is embraced as a primary form of evangelism, it puts things in perspective and counteracts some of the root causes of mission drift.

Studies shown that, in general, churches typically plateau in attendance by their fifteenth year, and by about thirty-five years they begin having trouble replacing the members they lose. Plus, the more established a church is, the older the average age of both its pastor and its people, often far older than the surrounding community—this is one more obstacle to evangelism. The fruit of conversions follows a similar pattern: among evangelical churches, those under three years old will win ten people to Christ per year for every hundred members. Those three to fifteen years old will win five people per year for every hundred members. After age fifteen the number drops to three per year."[7]

In short, the reason why church planting is the new evangelism today is the disproportionately high number of spiritual conversions experienced in new churches. When churches are "planted" (rather than just "started"), there is a soil of lostness in which the seed of the Gospel is sown.

Yet you could also say that this "new evangelism" is actually the old evangelism. It is rooted in the final words of Jesus on earth—his Great Commission mandate to make disciples by going, baptizing, and teaching (Matthew 28:19–20). These are church functions: only people like Robert Duvall in the 1998 movie *The Apostle* baptize themselves with no one else in community with them. The Great Commission is given to the church. When we baptize new believers "in the name of the Father and of the Son and of the Holy Spirit" (verse 19), we are incorporating them into the group of people who identify themselves by the name of the Father, Son, and Holy Spirit—in other words, the church. The story and practice of the early church,

The early church implemented the Great Commission mandate primarily by planting churches.

recorded in Acts, bears this out: the early church implemented the Great Commission mandate primarily by planting churches.

If the best indication of what Jesus meant can be found in how his hearers responded, as empowered and led by the Holy Spirit, then the early church fulfilled the Great Commission by planting churches. As they multiplied disciples they formed new congregations, who likewise reproduced themselves through other new churches.

Many churches have lost a church planting emphasis because they think it's no longer needed. After all, the thinking seems to be, there's a church on every corner and most of them are empty. Don't we already have enough churches? Don't we simply need to direct spiritually hungry people to those existing churches?

This sounds great in theory, but in reality it often doesn't work. New people are less likely to go to existing churches. Maybe they're overwhelmed by the prospect of breaking into the culture of an established congregation, especially if it's a long-standing group now in decline. Or perhaps outsiders have stereotyped existing churches, even if wrongly, deciding they're not relevant enough to today's culture? Maybe the church's reputation pushes them away. Certainly many have been scarred by a negative experience.

Whatever the case, churches are seeing the unique doors that a new church can often open and they are seeing the need for church planting again. They're relearning that church planting as the *new* evangelism has almost two thousands years of solid precedent!

Vision to Win the World—Through Church Planting

Most readers get regular e-mails from someone in Nigeria. Turns out they have some money for us. For lots of people that's all they know about Nigeria of late. They miss the thriving Anglican church, the Baptist conventions and the Methodist districts all doing remarkable things.

One of the world's fastest-spreading churches is the Redeemed Christian Church of God, a Pentecostal denomination started in Nigeria in 1952. If you haven't heard of them, you will in the coming years. In 2009 *Newsweek* magazine published a list of the fifty most powerful people in the world.[8] Joining President Barack Obama, Bill Gates, and Oprah Winfrey was the African pastor Enoch Adeboye, head of this new denomination of two million members that has already spread to 110 nations. (The Pope was the only other spiritual leader on the list.)

Warren heard that they're sending missionary church planters to the United States, so he drove to their U.S. headquarters, meeting with the head of the church's operations in North America.

It was a study in contrasts. Their North Texas office is a very simple building in the middle of a sorghum field, accessed by a gravel road in an unincorporated community of about one hundred people—none of them born in Nigeria, according to U.S. census data.

Yet the director's vision was limitless. "We must plan for at least 20,000 people to come to our annual North American church convention," my host explained with great enthusiasm. He showed me an architect's artistic rendering of what will happen "soon" on what turns out to be several hundred acres of adjoining fields that the church has bought. Patterned after the denomination's home base in Nigeria, the North Texas complex is informally called Redemption Camp and will become a gathering place for camp-style revivals and times of seeking God.

The church takes its purpose straight out of the Bible—to bring the Gospel to all nations, taking as many people as possible to heaven. This evangelistic focus is to be unfolded through a simple strategy, according to the church's website (www.rccgna .org): "we will plant churches within five minutes walking distance in every city and town of developing countries and within five minutes of driving distance in every city and town of developed countries."

That's a huge undertaking for a country the size and population of the United States. The first U.S. church began in Detroit in 1991 as a house fellowship of five people. By 2009 the denomination had four hundred U.S. churches with about fifteen thousand active members, most of them Nigerians.

"Did you locate your national office in Texas because it has more Nigerian-born residents than any other state?" Warren asked his host, having used www.peoplegroups.info to find out that information—20,927, according to the 2000 census.

"Our church is for *all* people," he responded immediately. He acknowledged that he and the other four people besides Warren in the building during my visit were Nigerian born. Then he affirmed that the church's goal is to make gradual inroads into the wider culture, moving to other immigrant groups and beyond. "Initially it may be rough," he said, "but some of our children grew up in America. They have white friends, they have African-American friends, and they have Asian friends. They will come to the church. It's a matter of time."

His passion is clear. The Redeemed Christian Church of God is highly organized worldwide in its church planting strategy and supervision, with this country as no exception. The leaders are passionate about seeing the power of God at work, transforming lives through Jesus Christ. For them, the planting of new churches—those that in turn reproduce—is the certain pathway to evangelism.

3

GROWTH BY MULTIPLICATION

Big Contrast to Addition

Leadership Network Numbers

- **New Churches Come from Many Quarters**

In the United States alone, at least sixty thousand churches were planted in the last twenty years. The majority came through the efforts of nondenominational groups and evangelical denominations. Maybe one out of eight were started by mainline denominations.[1]

- **Healthy Churches Reproduce**

The healthiest churches are those who reproduce, according to a national research project called FACT2008. Among the Protestant congregations surveyed, those whose leadership spent the most time recruiting and training other leaders were the healthiest. Similar results came from leaders who promoted a clear vision and emphasized evangelism. The massive survey factored in results from more than 2,000 randomly selected Protestant congregations.[2]

F"ive million church plants/One billion souls." That was the headline advertising a recent conference.[3] The goal was "to plant five million new churches and lead one billion people to Christ." Not a bad goal.

Ed was at the first meeting where this conversation started. There were fifty of us in the room. John Maxwell, James O. Davis, and Vonette Bright invited us to Orlando and told us that to "finish the task" of Bill Bright (which was really the task Jesus described in the Great Commission), we needed to do it through church planting. Bill Bright saw that pathway as did everyone in the room. At the conclusion of the meeting, they gave each of us a baton—a symbolic hand-off that the evangelical ministry of Bill Bright would be best fulfilled through the planting of churches.

Five million churches—that's no small vision. And these people are not just *talking* about church planting, they're *doing* some serious church planting. They're part of something really big that's taking place.

In recent decades, church planting was definitely not the admired choice that it is today. When Ed first told his parents that he was going to be a church planter, his dad asked, "So, no church was willing to hire you?" When Warren graduated from seminary and planted a church, his well-churched relatives kept affirming that they looked forward to the day when he'd serve "a real church." In recent years, attitudes have changed noticeably.

These days recent seminary grads have to be convinced to pastor an established church rather than to plant new ones. There is so much excitement about starting something new that some are voicing concern about the shortage of pastors for established churches.

Today energy and enthusiasm about church planting in North America is at an unprecedented high.

Today energy and enthusiasm about church planting in North America is at an unprecedented high. Now people are making T-shirts that say, "Church planting is for wimps. Reform an established church." Times have changed when you have to lure people away from planting. More church planting resources—books, funding, potential planters and sponsor churches—are available today than at any other time in history. More people are attending conferences on church planting. More seminaries are offering courses in church planting, a number having specific curriculum concentrations or even church planting centers. The net result is that the number of church planters is at an all-time high with the prospect of greater numbers to follow.

One example is the Exponential Conference (www.exponential conference.com), formally known as the National New Church Conference. Launched in its current form in 2006, it is a church planter's paradise. Everything a church planter could need is there—teaching on numerous topics, vendors selling everything needed for a new church, peer networking, and more. It is a conference by church planters for church planters, with church planters as the speakers.

If you had a national conference on new churches in 1990, you could have met in a garage. Today, it takes three thousand seats. The Exponential Conference has become the largest annual gathering of church planting leaders in North America—and possibly the world. Gatherings like this affirm that church planting has become mainstream.

How Do New Churches Best Extend the Kingdom of God?

Does church planting's new role as a mainstream option always guarantee good results? Not necessarily.

"The next big thing" in church always tends to comes in waves. In the 1980s, it was youth ministry. It seemed that everyone had to be a youth pastor talking about the culture and challenging kids to take their high schools for Christ. In the 1990s, it was Christian counseling. Everyone in ministry took on the title of counselor. Today, it's cool to be a church planter. All the real leaders are doing it. But is that really all that's needed?

Church planting is worthwhile only if it advances God's kingdom—God's area of reign in human hearts here on earth. When men and women are made into a "new creation" (2 Corinthians 5:17), it happens through a spiritual conversion. Thus, one way the kingdom is advanced is when new converts are made. Church planting has kingdom value only when it is focused on reaching the unchurched. (We also think that it advances God's kingdom when church plants make the world more like God wants it to be, but that will be addressed later in the book.)

> *Church planting is worthwhile only if it advances God's kingdom.*

Jesus said he came "to seek and to save the lost" (Luke 19:10). Churches old and new that reach lost people bring about the enlargement of God's kingdom. When new church plants do what they do best—make disciples—God's kingdom grows. God's Holy Spirit works in obedient hearts to multiply believers, just as the apostle Paul describes: "I planted the seed, Apollos watered it, but God made it grow" (1 Corinthians 3:6 NIV).

Luke describes Jesus sending seventy-two disciples to bless, heal, and announce that his kingdom is near. Upon hearing of their victories, even over demons, Jesus remarked that he "watched Satan fall from heaven like a lightning flash" (Luke 10:18). When the church advances, the forces of darkness recede. So here's an important question: is your congregation advancing through the dark territories?

It's very possible to plant a church but not enlarge God's kingdom or to limit Satan's domain. Churches based on worship preferences and musical styles, or built around celebrities within the Christian subculture, reinforce consumerism and promote church shopping among those who are already believers.

Our friend Andy Crouch, author of *Culture Making*, told this story in a *Christianity Today* article, describing a short conversation he had with a twenty-five-year-old pastor wearing distressed jeans, multiple piercings, and a pricey hairstyle. The pastor told Andy:

> "We're starting a church for cool people."
> "Cool people?"
> "Yeah, you know, people like us."
> (He doesn't mean himself and me; he means himself and his friends—all of whom do indeed exude a level of coolness about which I could only dream.)[4]

That same conversation could have occurred with someone of any age. To be sure, everyone needs the kind of community found in a church. Even cool people do—people like us (OK, not really *us*, because we work in research). But the greatest motive behind church planting is not simply to create an environment for people "just like us" so that we can have a comfortable place with each other. The goal is to advance the kingdom of God through the planting of churches that give God glory, honor, and praise.

If such churches reach cool people, that's great. But to do kingdom work we also have to reach people we don't view as cool, including people that nobody views as cool.

Currently we are seeing an uptick in the number of ethnic church plants. We applaud these efforts, but what do we do about the second, third, and fourth generation immigrant groups that don't identify with those churches? We live in a multilayered society. The increasing influence of globalization and urbanization, combined with technology-assisted grouping of people around affinities, highlight the need for an increase of multicultural churches capable of handling diverse ethnicities, economic backgrounds, and spiritual backgrounds.

Overall, a church multiplication movement will mean more churches like yours, and like Ed's and Warren's, but also communities and networks of healthy and Gospel-focused churches completely different from ours. To truly reach our world, churches need to multiply among every thin slice of society: suburban, urban, rural, cowboy, artistic, senior adult, collegiate—and on the list goes. These groups each have their own language, culture, values, and perspectives. If a biblical church effectively reaches any of the varied members of the human race, we're in favor of it.

Does Church Planting Mean Multiplication?

The purpose of this book is to do far more than to cheer for and legitimate church planting. Our "viral church" idea is about falling in love with multiplication and abandoning what seems to be an addiction to addition.

We're both friends with a pastor named Ralph Moore, and not just because his church is in Hawaii, where Warren has visited twice (and Ed, staying home, wrote the foreword to Ralph's newest book). Previously Ralph pastored in Hermosa Beach, California, where Warren also visited.

Far more significant than his idyllic locations is the way in which Ralph's ministry has multiplied. Here's how his résumé might summarize everything that has happened since 1971, when he first became a pastor:

1. Started one youth group.
2. Planted two churches.
3. Had a direct hand in multiplying over seventy church plants from the congregations that he pastored.
4. By 2010 the impact through replication had spanned seven hundred churches on six continents, representing more than 100,000 people.

Somewhere along the way, the multiplication took off. The churches he's helped birth have almost become a movement that keeps generating new congregations. Now it's out of control—at least largely out of *his* control.

Maybe the best way to illustrate Ralph's belief in multiplication as superior to addition is to describe something crazy that he did. If you visit his church location today, you would barely notice the modest buildings. Instead you'd be in awe about the gigantic, towering mountain just a few feet outside the back windows. Ralph's church facilities literally back up into a mountain that rises so sharply that it looks like the street-level entrance to a thousand-foot skyscraper. And in fact there's a very good reason for that situation: their property was literally carved out of a mountain.

Terracing a mountain was a very creative way of finding ten acres of available property, but the church's approach created another problem—serious rainwater runoff. When they first built the place, they needed something that would grow quickly as ground cover to prevent any soil from washing away.

The church decided the best groundcover was a plant that had only recently been introduced to Hawaii. A four-inch pot was selling for nearly five dollars at the time. "Our best estimate was that we needed 200,000 of these plants at a cost approximating a million dollars," Ralph told me. Being a strong believer in the idea of multiplication, Ralph and his congregation came up with a creative plan. It involved the backyard at Ralph's home.

"I killed off a twenty-by-twenty-foot section of lawn and planted just thirteen of those expensive plants," he explained. "They were all the nursery had in stock. We then multiplied them by taking cuttings from the mother plants."

A few weeks later they took more cuttings from their newly pruned and rapidly growing groundcover. A group of college kids from the church took over the task, eventually harvesting nearly a quarter of a million individual plants from that backyard patch.

Those plants, in turn, filled in well enough to cover the entire church campus. It saved major dollars, plus it gave a living lesson in the power of multiplication.

How Ralph Multiplies at Church

Ralph's multiplication emphasis with people is almost as simple as what he did with the plants. His first priority during each week is to disciple his staff. Often they'll read the same book and then they'll discuss it in a weekly staff meeting. They pray and minister to each other in the same meeting. It usually lasts a couple of hours and currently happens on Tuesdays.

That discipleship emphasis happens before they do necessary business, such as figuring out what to do with two groups both wanting the church van at the same time, planning how the upcoming men's retreat will be promoted, and discussing why the community service initiative got such a big response. "I think discipling the staff is as important as preparing a message and certainly more important than any day-to-day planning," Ralph says. One of the principles Ralph has embraced for church multiplication is that leadership development is always worth your time. In fact, it is one of the best ways to spend your time. As you will see in the following paragraphs, it is a lesson he has successfully passed on to others.

Leadership development is always worth your time. In fact, it is one of the best ways to spend your time.

The staff, in turn, spend most of their time discipling volunteer leaders of what are called "MiniChurches." A MiniChurch is a group of about a dozen people who gather weekly to share what the Holy Spirit said to them during the weekend sermon, to share life experiences, and to pray for each other. They also eat lots of sweets!

The term MiniChurch refers to a small-group experience as a miniature church. The idea is to model the first-century church that early Christians experienced before the establishment of institutionalized denominations. In the New Testament era Christians met in homes where they could be with their extended spiritual family in a warm personal setting, safely exercise spiritual gifts, stretch their faith, and sharpen one another as "iron sharpens iron" (Proverbs 27:17).

MiniChurches meet weekly to review the Bible teaching from the weekend services. The format is simple and reproducible as participants ask: What did you learn? (head), What did God say to you? (heart), and What will you do? (hands). Church staff disciple the MiniChurch leaders in a similar way—by reading books together or by operating as a MiniChurch made up of leaders. The MiniChurch leaders in turn all have apprentice leaders whom they disciple. Then the leaders and their apprentices together disciple the members of their MiniChurches. "Any church that focuses on disciplemaking is by definition going to be a more authentic church," Ralph affirmed.

Where did Ralph find a staff who can do that? The MiniChurch discipleship chain produces nearly all the church's staff pastors. Each year, it also produces one or two pastors capable of planting a new church. Those individuals receive encouragement to develop their gifts further by starting a new church.

"It is all pretty simple," Ralph said. "It may look a little different in every congregation, but we keep coming back to the MiniChurch as *the* place to start. From there we can go in any direction." Some MiniChurches multiply quickly like rabbits and others develop more slowly or grow larger before they multiply, more like the twenty-two months of gestation an elephant typically requires. "We support both the rapid multiplication of rabbit churches or the slower growth and reproduction of elephants," Ralph said. "We want to be an 'and' church, not an 'or' group."

The gist of Ralph's passion is that by multiplying groups locally, and by steadily and strategically planting new churches that, in turn, plant new churches, the global church creates more of what he calls "harvest points." That translates to more lives changed for Jesus Christ and a greater good for the places where those people live.

"Harvest points" is a great descriptor of what Ralph's church is producing and what you must embrace to witness a church multiplication movement. Ed is on the road a lot and meets hundreds of church planters each year. One of the temptations which each planter faces when launching a new church or network of churches is to simply reproduce or even clone their current look and feel. The logic seems to make sense: "We have an effective model here and they need it there." But Ralph's mentality has been to create harvest points which are unique to each environment. The passion he lives, models, and produces in others is to create a place of spiritual birth rather than religious mimicry. If you will make this adjustment in your heart and the heart of your church, then a multiplying movement will become closer to reality.

Ralph's church has planted several new churches in Hawaii and even more in other states and countries. One of the churches he helped plant has multiplied itself into over a hundred others. Another church he helped plant is up to nine generations. Ralph has influenced the planting of churches all around the world because he focuses on multiplication, not addition.

Many congregations and pastors measure their health by whether their church is growing. To Ralph, that's the wrong metric. The better measurement is whether their people are learning to reproduce themselves. Ralph calls it "disciples multiplying churches." It represents a profound shift in ministry, one that few churches and even fewer church plants

The better measurement is whether their people are learning to reproduce themselves.

have made. But it forms the kind of church that's able to multiply and then do so on multiple occasions.

Conventional wisdom for the church is the opposite of Ralph's metric. In seminary, many of us learned the metric of "churches multiplying disciples." Though it is a noble goal, it will never result in massive multiplication. The emphasis is on changing one life at a time, slowly and incre-

> *The metric of "churches multiplying disciples" will never result in massive multiplication.*

mentally. We measure addition because, at its core, it is a metric built upon the ability to control the situation. Well-intentioned people will slow or squelch a multiplication movement by pursuing "quality," waiting for "maturity," or insisting on adherence to the existing organizational structure.

With "disciples multiplying church," you are inviting the unknown. It is the place where the person in the pew, chair, or theater seat is given permission—or, better stated, given marching orders—to go and change the world by starting a new church. When you allow this idea to invade your congregation, God will raise up leaders from corners of the congregation that you never expected and who will do more than you ever imagined.

Ralph believes the New Testament norm is for you and me to *multiply* our congregations. Church multiplication carries the potential for exponential growth of the Gospel.

Why Do We Add, Rather Than Multiply?

Why don't more churches multiply? The quick answers are: their leaders have not thought of it, they don't know how, and it seems too difficult. Ultimately, though, it's because they don't understand the importance of doing so. Perhaps it's because they don't see multiplication clearly enough in the pages of our Bibles.

One approach is to examine what Jesus did. He replicated himself in his disciples and gave them his authority to do the things he did. He taught them by on-the-job training. He said that through the Holy Spirit they would do "even greater things" than what he did on earth (see John 14:12).

Jesus had three close disciples that he especially poured himself into. Not one but three, then a circle of twelve around them, and then a circle of seventy around that. Should a multiple-apprentice approach like that be a model for Christian leaders today? Should we affirm to those we train that God may well be raising them up to do "even greater things" than they have seen in the ministry of those who train them?

When Jesus sent out a group of his disciples in pairs, part of their assignment was to find someone local in each town (Luke 10:6), and then to heal the sick and preach about the kingdom of God. These disciples, who are much like today's church planters, were then to nimbly move on, presumably leaving their contact in charge—the local person they've been discipling as someone to pastor the new congregation. This paradigm fosters rapid multiplication and it is also easy to replicate.

The paradigm also begs a question: how long does it take to disciple a person? The real turning point is to know when someone is ready to lead. If a church multiplication movement is to emerge, our disciple-making strategy must be characterized in two ways: intentional and full of faith. By intentional, we mean the planter must immediately and intentionally invest into those who will be the next leaders. You must make the decision that they are worth every effort you can give them. Second, our disciple-making must be full of faith. Not in the person we're discipling but in the divine Person to whom they belong. Don't get caught in the trap of thinking you have to stay until they are 100 percent ready. None of us were 100 percent ready when we planted our first church and neither will any of your followers be. Instead, trust that as God prepared and steadied you through the process, he will do the same for them. By showing confidence in them, they will show confidence in those God raises up after you are gone.

Is the implication for churches that we need an approach to evangelism that centers on church multiplication instead of addition? As our friend Ralph Moore often says, "It's time to stop counting converts and begin counting congregations."

> *"It's time to stop counting converts and begin counting congregations."*
>
> —RALPH MOORE

How to Move Toward Multiplication

If multiplication is a central New Testament pattern and it offers so many benefits, then why do so many of us have a hard time advancing beyond an addition mentality? Maybe because it's more difficult. It can be hard to figure out how to build genuine multiplication into a church. Simple addition seems easier.

One of Ralph's most recent books is *How to Multiply Your Church*. Warren was asked to write an endorsement for it and, as previously mentioned, Ed was asked to write the foreword. In the foreword, Ed talked about one of the classic episodes of Star Trek named "The Trouble with Tribbles." On that particular voyage of the starship Enterprise, the crew encountered some lovable little fuzzballs called Tribbles. At first, the crew was fascinated with these cute little creatures. Then everything changed when they overwhelmed the vessel through rapid multiplication. Tribbles multiplied faster than rabbits. Why? Because they were born pregnant. What a great goal for every church plant!

That vivid episode shows how dramatically multiplication changes things. It also reminds us that today's world of church planting is still one largely of addition thinking—which will only perpetuate church-as-usual with the current outcome that too few people are being touched by a vibrant, Christ-like community. Addition is a good thing, and certainly better than nothing. But to really change things, we need to learn how to multiply churches.

In the "Tribbles" episode, the crew of the ship eventually sought out a way to end the multiplying reproduction of the Tribbles. Though the crew found the Tribbles cute at first, ultimately they were overwhelmed by the number that appeared—thus the name of the episode, "The *Trouble* with Tribbles." The interesting twist in the episode occurs when the Tribbles become the heroes by uncovering a dastardly plot by the enemies. The creature which seemed to be a bane was discovered to be a blessing.

We need the same value shift to take place among established churches today. We want to lift up church planting multipliers as heroes of church leadership in our day. These are the leaders who will lead the charge delivering defeat to our enemy and victory for the newly born again. But in order for that to happen, two things must occur.

First, church multiplication must be lauded as a worthy and achievable goal by those not in the middle of it. Instead of seeing church multiplication movement leaders as a vermin to eradicate, generous help and support should go to them as they plow new ground for new orchards. We need denominational leaders on local and national levels to applaud the work of leaders who seek to multiply churches. Plus they need to do it loudly and publicly.

Second, we hope to see church planters become church multipliers. Without any hesitation, all church planters can make the commitment for this change in mentality. Perhaps it will take assessment and training (we discuss those issues in a later chapter), but all church planters can work toward multiplying churches through their own or through a network committed to a multiplying effect.

In the foreword to *How to Multiply Your Church*, Ed asked what a new world of multiplication might look like—what would happen if our churches grew like Tribbles. What will it take to change our world from one of addition to one of multiplication? Ed concluded that first we must get ourselves, our egos, and especially our current puny thinking out of the way. Second, we must ask God for several increases in our lives and our churches:

1. *Bigger Faith.* When was the last time you asked God to do something in your life or in the life of your church that makes his name and fame great. That's what the disciples asked of Jesus, "Increase our faith!" (Luke 17:5). For some, just thinking about reproduction and multiplication is like asking them to give extreme skiing or bungee jumping a try. For this type of movement to take place in your life, you must unleash yourself from a pedestrian faith that makes God seem so small. Ask for epic-sized faith. We need to ask, "What does God want?"

2. *Greater Focus on Jesus.* John the Baptizer said, "He must increase, but I must decrease" (John 3:30). If you think about it, John had a pretty good thing going. Aside from a weird diet and unfashionable dress, he had lots of people coming to him. He had a big following, and he was all about a smackdown on the religious leaders. What a gig! But once Jesus arrived on the scene, John pointed people solely in Jesus' direction. John even encouraged those following him to follow Jesus. John could no longer be center stage as he talked about the coming Messiah. Now Jesus had come and Jesus' kingdom was the issue. Your church planting network is not about your church or its methodology. It is about Jesus the Great High Priest who has come to reconcile sinful and broken people back to God. We need to be reminded, "Who is this all about?"

3. *Fresh Boldness in Sharing God's Word.* The book of Acts repeatedly talks about the boldness of the believers (4:31; 9:28; 13:46; 14:3; 18:26; and 19:8). Likewise the book of Acts repeatedly reports how the church grew and spread, such as Acts 12:24 NIV: "But the Word of God continued to increase and spread." Is there a relationship between the two? The Word of God is increasing and spreading in other parts of the world right now. The last two verses of Acts show the power of God's Word. It says, "Then he stayed two whole years in his own rented house. And he welcomed all who visited him, proclaiming the kingdom of God and teaching

the things concerning the Lord Jesus Christ with full bold-
ness and without hindrance" (Acts 28:30–31). In the midst of
Rome's pagan empire, Paul had no problems speaking God's
Word about man's Savior. A good question is, "Why not in
North America, again?"

4. *Overflowing and Expanding Love.* Multiplying disciples and
   churches requires a special kind of love for Jesus, for the church
   Jesus started, and for the lost peoples around the world who
   need the spiritual community a church can provide. Paul
   prayed that the church at Thessalonica would direct God's love
   to those in their world. As The Message words it, "And may
   the Master pour on the love so it fills your lives and splashes
   over on everyone around you, just as it does from us to you.
   May you be infused with strength and purity, filled with confidence in the presence of God our Father when our Master
   Jesus arrives with all his followers" (1 Thessalonians 3:12–13;
   Message). It's good to ask ourselves, "How are you praying?"

Addition is a good thing, and certainly far better than nothing.
For churches that have moved from seeing no one come to faith last
year to one person this year, we rejoice. For the established church
that has decided to plant its very first new church, we get excited.
But to really change things, we need
to learn how to *multiply* churches.

> *To really change things,
> we need to learn how to
> multiply churches.*

All ministry is costly. Personal
evangelism takes time, effort, and
some risk. Planting a church means
people, resources, and money are
leaving the congregation. These are short-term losses that we trust
are replaced by healthy believers and churches as they trust God's
provisions. A church multiplication movement will cost you even
more. But it is a cost worth paying.

What is interesting, though, is that it will become habitual.
Ralph Moore no longer knows how to operate without starting
new churches on a consistent basis. He and his congregations

have grown accustomed to the chaos, shifting, sending, and cost involved with such a movement. Even more than being accustomed to it—they like it. Why? Because through the movement, they are seeing lives saved in their own community and around the world. For church multiplication to become mainstream, only one thing needs to happen: you need to do it. Perhaps then we will see a flood of new faces come into the frame ready to send more than they are able and give more than they have so that we can all see God do more than we can imagine.

4

NEW PLAYERS

Aggressive Local Churches and Church Planting Networks

Leadership Network Numbers

- **Church Sponsoring Benefits the Sponsor as Well**

   A study of church-sponsoring churches showed that the typical sponsor fared quite well from the experience. Worship attendance increased 22 percent for the five years after sponsorship of the church plant. Financial giving to the local church likewise increased 48 percent over that same period, and designated gifts such as toward foreign missions giving increased 77 percent.[1]

- **Funding of New Churches Has Shifted to More Local Levels**

   According to our "State of Church Planting USA" research, the majority of funding for new churches increasingly rests on the parent church and church planter, with the denomination providing no more than 33 percent of needed funds.[2]

- **More Denominational Funding Means Less Sponsorship Locally**

   There appears to be a trended correlation between the amount of money the national agency contributes to each church plant and the number of parent churches in that denomination. More money from the national agency correlates with a lower percentage of parent churches.[3]

Shortly after the United States won its war for independence, people began moving westward in great numbers. The population shift was massive—regions that had been virtually uninhabited in 1776 contained one-third of the nation's population by 1790.[4] Wherever they went, a remarkable church planting movement swept through the American frontier. It resulted in multiple churches in virtually every county, city, town, and hamlet that settlers inhabited. The planting of new churches occurred at a rate that is almost unbelievable, especially because the blitz of church planting had no central hub.

The clear winners of the western frontier were the Baptists and Methodists. The most striking change of all was the growth of the Methodists from thirty small societies in 1776 to nearly 20,000 congregations in 1860 (see Table 4.1). Baptists, which were the second-largest denominational group by 1860, continued to grow, passing the Methodists in size before 1900. Today they are the largest Protestant faith group—far larger than the New England–based Congregationalists that were the first to colonize this country (see Table 4.2), and pioneered the efforts of missionary work both among Native Americans and among Europeans who went west and north to unsettled areas.

Table 4.1: Dramatic Historic Growth of Various Denominations (by Number of Churches)[5]

Denomination	1776	1860
Methodist societies	30	19,833
Baptist	380	11,221
Presbyterian	300	5,061
Roman Catholic	52	2,550
Congregational	700	2,234
Church of England and Protestant Episcopal	300	2,145
Lutheran	60	2,128
Christian Church and Disciples of Christ	0	2,068

Table 4.2: Baptists Far Outpaced the Original Congregationalists (by Number of Churches)[6]

Denomination	1750	1850	1950
Congregationalist (New England)	600	1,600	3,200
Methodist (frontier)	0	1,200	5,800
Baptist (frontier)	200	8,600	77,000

The explosive growth of new churches, particularly between 1795 and 1810, is the only true church planting movement (as missiologist David Garrison defines such movements) to occur on the soil of what is now the United States. During those fifteen years, some three thousand churches were started, according to *The Churching of America*.[7] Is there any reason why we could not see the impact of those fifteen years repeated during our lifetime?

This massive church planting phenomenon has not yet happened again in the United States—although some might argue that Pentecostalism's U.S. expansion during the last century was similar among certain social groups. Yet a similar massive church planting *has* occurred in recent history in numerous developing nations around the world. In 1999 Garrison collected reports of potential church planting movements from various countries and wrote an internal report for the Southern Baptist International Mission Board titled "Church Planting Movements." It became so widely read that it was formally published in 2003.[8] Garrison has continued to research the topic and has become a world authority on it.

According to Garrison, a church planting movement "is a rapid and multiplicative increase of indigenous churches planting churches within a given people group or population segment."[9] That concept translates into reports from all quarters of the developing world, such as

- From Ethiopia: "After the new believers/leaders are baptized, they are so on fire that we simply cannot hold them back.

They fan out all over the country starting Bible studies, and a few weeks later we begin to get word back how many have started. It's the craziest thing we ever saw! We did not start it, and we couldn't stop it if we tried."

- From one city in China: "Over a four-year period (1993–1997), more than 20,000 people came to faith in Christ, resulting in more than 500 new churches."

While doing the research that led to this book, Ed collaborated with David Garrison and wrote a research paper that we have adapted in this chapter. As they discussed church planting movements around the world and also the one that occurred two centuries ago here in North America, they considered an important question: Why haven't we experienced another one in North America since then? Is the answer due to external factors beyond our control, such as a huge population migration, or is it simply that nobody in this country has tried to create the environment necessary for another church planting movement? This is a great question that we are hoping to answer.

We believe that a movement *could* occur today and that one vital ingredient is lay empowerment at a local church level. It may not be exactly a church planting movement as per David's definition, but we do believe it can be what we're calling a church multiplication movement. That is, back in the heyday of 1795 to 1810, all you needed to be a church planter was a godly lifestyle and a congregation that would give you permission to do so. (In the concluding chapter of this book we again revisit Garrison's question

> *A church multiplication movement today would be characterized by a 50 percent conversion rate (new believers) and a 50 percent reproduction rate (new churches) sustained for at least three generations of churches.*

and offer additional answers.) If church multiplication like that happened again today, it would be characterized by a 50 percent conversion rate (new believers) and a 50 percent reproduction rate (new churches) sustained for at least three generations of churches (parent, child, grandchild). Thus, as we explain more in the opening chapter of *Viral Churches*, each church will plant another new church every other year on average, all with at least half the participants as new followers of Jesus Christ.

Why the Movement Ended

Historians tend to use labels like "The Great Century of Missions" for the 1800s, which included so many rapidly multiplying churches. Their focus is mostly on all the mission agencies which began and proliferated during that era.[10] History books and encyclopedias acknowledge the role that lay preachers played, but few have taken a close look as to why the lay church planting movement on the ever-expanding western frontier was so powerful. These "unpaid local amateurs"[11] were a wave of homegrown, minimally trained church planters, themselves often relatively new believers. Yet, they were essential for the multiplication to occur. Thanks to a climate that validated lay leadership, along with simple models for training them, that era became the most successful lay church planting movement in American history—thus far. All of it happened by simply accessing the available pool of leaders available at the time. As one historian wrote about the Methodist approach to church planting:

> It is doubtful if a missionary system better adapted to the needs of the frontier in the early part of the nineteenth century could have been found. . . . The settlements were widely scattered; the people generally had not the means, and frequently not the desire, to call and settle ministers in their midst. The circuit rider did not wait for a call—he sought the people. Church buildings were rarely found,

but that did not hinder the work of the itinerant; the cabin of a friendly settler would do at the outset. . . . The Methodist circuit riders were the advance guard of American Christianity in the occupation of the West.[12]

There are two lessons that we can point out from these observations. First, the circuit riders sought the people. As we watch churches who are initiating multiplying movements, they are, if nothing else, aggressive in reaching out to new people. Their leaders bore easily of ministry that is preservation focused or lacking in challenge. In fact, they are driven to the edge of insanity by maintenance mode. Leaders of great movements are those driven to find new people and carry them into a new future. In church planting, that means searching for one more person to plant one more church so they can reach one more city or demographic group.

Another lesson we discover from frontier ministers is their willingness to pay the price that accompanies great ministry. Circuit riders were the "special forces" of ministry in their day. In many ways, church planters hold that position today on the American continent. As we hope to participate in a great movement of God, it will take great personal effort. The champions of multiplying movements are intentionally stepping into their roles and expending their lives for a great cause. As J. Oswald Sanders, a leader with Overseas Missionary Fellowship, wrote, "Fatigue is the price of leadership. Mediocrity is the result of never getting tired."[13]

Circuit riders of yesteryear were legendary for their pioneering spirit. A humorous expression on days of bad weather was, "There's nobody out today but crows and Methodist preachers."[14]

Each of the Methodist circuits included twenty to thirty preaching points. Worship services were generally held in whatever facilities were available—even outside. Buildings were not necessary for churches on the frontier. Pastors used any place that people would gather together—"in the open, in homes, saloons, gambling halls, and under brush arbors."[15]

Obviously, the circuit rider was unable to shepherd this number of preaching points. Class presidents—usually "farmer-preachers"—served as the under-shepherds. They were the ones who actually led the congregation.

Likewise Baptists grew because of their "genius for making Baptists out of the raw materials which the frontier afforded."[16] As a denomination, Baptists had no enduring evangelistic program until the start of the nineteenth century.[17] They didn't have to ask permission of anyone; the "farmer-preachers"[18] just went out and started new churches. Their licensed ministers frequently served in much the same way that the "local" or "lay" preachers among the Methodists served: they preached more or less at large.[19] For frontier Baptists the calling process was as follows:

> When a "brother" was impressed that God had called him to preach, he made it known to the church and if, after the church had heard the trial sermon, it approved of his "gifts" a license was then given him to preach in a small territory, as for instance within the bounds of a single church. After further trail, if his "gifts" proved real, and he gave further evidence of usefulness as a preacher he was then permitted to preach within the bounds of the association. If, on the other hand, his "gifts" as a preacher did not seem to improve he was advised to make no further attempts to preach.[20]

Most pastors in the West were bivocational, often entirely unremunerated, devoting only a fraction of their time to ministry and often dividing that among several churches.[21] Educated clergy were the exception during this time.[22] Preaching was affective and emotional. Lay preaching was the order of the day. Extemporaneous preaching was valued above prepared sermons.[23]

In these descriptions, we see the value of contextualization during the 1800s church planting movement. The planters and pastors of the west did not have congregants with university degrees and highly educated communities. Each day, they sought to reach farmers, cattle ranchers, and cowboys. To do so, they tailored their methodology to the sociology. And they did so without research firms and Excel reports of population trends. How? By living among the community rather than existing within a religious subculture. Multiplying movements are born from the impulse of the missionary, not the monastic.

Multiplying movements are born from the impulse of the missionary, not the monastic.

The Methodist and Baptist systems had different terms but were remarkably similar in function. Methodists tended to form a "class" before a church. Baptists followed a similar pattern, forming what McBeth calls "fellowship groups" before forming churches. The Methodists were organized in circuits. The Baptists created associations of multiple churches in the same geographic area.[24] Both the Methodist and Baptists were locally run. This empowered people on the frontier to be involved in every segment of church life—from church discipline, to worship, to preaching, and on limited occasions, to the exercise of the ordinances.

What effect did all this lay leadership have? It typically became a new church, a portion of whom were new believers—a process replicated literally thousands of times. Take one of the United Methodist churches in still-rural Caswell County, North Carolina. It started in 1779, which means it has been organized longer than the denomination to which it belongs. So it started before rules and procedures had been formalized—the first Methodist pastors were not ordained as ministers until after 1783. Though most likely scandalous to some, ultimately these leaders were a joy to the lost and a catalyst for action to the saved.

The congregation traces its beginnings to the emphasis that created many Methodist churches during that era: class meetings. They involved reading Scripture and listening to sermons by lay ministers. A dozen or more people, typically family members and neighbors in the immediate area, would attend the meetings, which initially convened under a big oak tree. Class meetings then moved to the lay leader's home. The class meeting developed into a church, adding singing, testimonies, and children's ministry to its weekly activities. Eventually members built a log church near the church's current location.

Many members of this church today can trace their spiritual lineage to the man who led those early meetings. The church facility today has the classic look of a white clapboard country church. It has a long history of members seeking to be faithful to God and to serve God in the community. It has met a need and continues to do so, although it has not reproduced itself through other churches.

This story is typical of many churches in that era: a person came to faith, received training, began traveling as an evangelist or itinerant preacher, started an embryo church, left it in the hands of someone else, and continued on to start new churches. This movement continued until those churches stopped reproducing and stopped sending out their own missionaries. By that point, denominations were formed and formalized to organize and ideally continue the outreach and growth. But we must remember that the denominations exist to aid the church. When the attitude is reversed, then uncompromising preservation becomes the goal rather than exponential expansion.

It is interesting to note that during this era, the American Home Mission Society sent out many trained workers, but even with the support of mainline denominations, it made little headway against the Baptists and Methodists. Likewise The Missionary Society of Connecticut was formed in 1798 to "Christianize the Heathen in North America, and to support and promote Christian Knowledge in the new settlements within the United States." (Ed and Warren are very curious as to the public reaction if a network or denomination used the word "heathen" in its vision statement today.) By 1801, fifteen missionaries were appointed by the society. The Massachusetts Missionary Society, founded in 1799, had a similar mission. Other agencies followed—each sent out a handful of missionaries to the West, with generally little response.

The Baptists and Methodists were different. These frontier pastors did not generally go *as* missionaries. They went in search of economic opportunity that the West provided.[25] As they *went*, they were, or *became*, the missionaries. The vast majority of home missions in the late 1700s were conducted by these figures.

> *As they* went, *they were, or* became, *the missionaries.*

For those readers who are bivocational planters and pastors, take heart. You have a great heritage. Many of your predecessors were the leaders used by God to conquer the wild heart of the western frontier. We're glad to know that leaders like you are ready to work like those in your community for fifty hours a week and still "gut it out" to plant a church ready to plant more churches. We think you are some of our greatest warriors for the faith.

As Baptists, Methodists, and other frontier church groups eventually formalized denominations, they often became less focused on reaching new people. Instead more energy went to maintaining existing churches. In the process, attitudes changed from valuing the launch of new churches to asking, "Why not just help to strengthen and grow the churches we already have?"

This is another important question. Because that is not the purpose of this book, we will make our answer brief. Planting churches and revitalizing churches is not a choice we must make between two ideals. Rather it is choice we must make to *fulfill* two ideals. On the one hand, if you are interested in leading a movement from an established church, then help your people see the possibilities that lie ahead. Don't be surprised to see a revitalization of that established church. On the other hand, if you have no core group, no building, but a heart for a city or a group of people, then strike out with all the faith you can summon and watch as God calls up laborers to go with you.

There is also a kingdom issue at stake. In an ideal world, the new church will draw 100 percent of its people from the ranks of the unchurched. More realistically, a new church will draw *most* of their new members (maybe 50 percent) from the ranks of the unchurched, with some of the rest coming from existing churches. That is probably inevitable. At this point, the existing churches need to examine their kingdom motivations, asking: "Will we rejoice in the 50 percent—the new people that the kingdom has gained through this new church, or will we bemoan and resent the families we lost to it?" In other words, do churches care more about their own institutional turf or about the overall health and prosperity of the kingdom of God in their area?

Any church that is more upset by its own small losses rather than the kingdom's large gains is betraying its narrow interests.

The Need for New Players

Today, unfortunately, the church planting movement across all denominations has not only long since stopped, but among United Methodists and numerous other denominations, more churches close each year than open. Denominational churches are not alone. The average nondenominational and "quasi-denominational" church also tends to launch, take root, and then, well, not grow too much.

Thus for the overall Protestant landscape of America, most congregations today are small, according to Duke Divinity School researcher Mark Chaves, who directs the National Congregations Study, a major survey of houses of worship across religious lines. He reports that the median congregation has only 75 regularly participating people and an annual budget of approximately $90,000. Ninety percent of all congregations have 350 or fewer people.

While megachurches and fast-growing churches grab headlines, they are comparatively few in number. Megachurches, defined as congregations with average attendances of two thousand or more adults and children, represent 0.4 percent of the total Protestant church population (although they draw almost 10 percent of all worshipers).[26]

We like megachurches—well, many of them! Some of our best friends lead them. At the time of this writing, Ed has been preaching at one every week for the last two years and Warren was on staff for eleven years with a church as its congregation grew from eight hundred to two thousand. But we believe they are but one possible solution to reaching our culture for Christ. Ultimately, we need far more churches than we currently have in order to reach our ever-expanding and diversifying culture.

Among churches of all sizes, growing churches are rare. In fact, they only make up about 20 percent of our churches today. The other 80 percent have reached a plateau or are declining. Perhaps a change in mission—like the thrust to plant new churches—can revitalize the spirit of many existing churches.

Today, in addition to church planting networks, aggressive local churches—some using the label "apostolic"—are beginning to fill the gap and create a new momentum. One that has a bit of history to it is what is known today as the Association of Vineyard Churches. Ed had the privilege of spending two days with the national leadership of the Vineyard in 2009. The movement is still aggressively involved in church planting. However, it was much more so in the past (and the desire to reclaim that focus is why they asked him to their meeting).

At its growth peak, the leaders of the Vineyard explained that they were only planting at a 75 percent rate. In other words, this means that if the association had one hundred churches one year, it started seventy-five more churches the next year.

How did that rapid-church multiplication happen? Carol Wimber, widow of the founder, recently looked back on the movement and explained how she saw God work: "If you were a Christian and God had worked in your life, you had a job to do! . . . These people might have been in church only two weeks, but if they understood their call, they knew they had something to share with everyone they met—with the whole world. . . . They led so many people to the Lord in that way."[27] Today's attitude of church membership and mission is vastly different. A return to the *salvation* = *call* = *obedience* equation of the Christian life will have a dramatic impact on your church's chances of seeing a multiplying movement occur.

Are denominations continuing to plant churches? Absolutely, with many ramping up their commitment. But we must never forget the Ephesians 3:10 lesson from Paul that God chose the church as the place to reveal himself to the nations.

Though ecclesiastical organizations can serve a great benefit to a church, God did not establish any denominations or networks; churches create them to help accomplish the mission God gave the church. It is the church that will crash through the gates of hell and rescue those bound in sin and hurtling toward judgment. Denominations truly making a difference in the kingdom are those who foster environments that welcome true leaders, plan for multiplying growth, and celebrate new churches.

Take the International Pentecostal Holiness Church, the third-largest Pentecostal denomination and in the same family as the Assemblies of God and the Church of God (Cleveland). It currently has just over 2,000 churches in the United States. In a four-year period (2004–2008) it planted 395 new churches. That represents 93 percent of the net new membership of the denomination during that period. In a ten-year period (1998–2008) it started 1,157 churches. That's an average of 115 new churches per year, more than a 10 percent annual growth rate. These gains are among the highest in the history of the denomination since its founding in 1895.

One way they've planted so many churches is through a mother-church effort which they call the Antioch Network. This is a thrust to cast a vision, provide training, and build a national network for pastors who desire to birth a new church from their existing congregation.

The one persistent problem that continues to plague the church planting effort of the International Pentecostal Holiness Church—but by no means unique to that denomination—is the church closure rate. During the same four years of its 395 new churches, it closed 396 churches representing a loss of 24,001 members. The large number of new churches annually and the net increase in membership they represent ensure continued growth for the denomination, but the problem of an unacceptably high closure rate must be resolved.[28]

The Vineyard and International Pentecostal Holiness Church are not alone in their church planting efforts. There are other definite leaders of the pack. The best practitioners among church planting networks include Glocalnet, Stadia, and Acts 29. Each of these leaders has developed strong systems, methods, and results. The best practitioners among denominations include both mainline and evangelical examples. Among mainline denominations with strong church planting emphases are the Lutheran Church—Missouri Synod and the Reformed Church in America. Among evangelical denominations are Converge (formerly, the Baptist General Conference), the Evangelical Covenant Church, the Missionary Church, Assemblies of God, the Nazarenes, and Presbyterian Church in America. Each of these groups has well-developed systems and programs with effective results.

Christ the King Is Out of Control

When Warren first met Dave Browning, founder of Christ the King Community Church International, in Mt. Vernon, Washington, he immediately sensed him to be a man of great vision. He's laid back, wearing jeans every time Warren met him, but he radiates an energy and passion that are contagious. When he later visited his church facility, sixty miles north of Seattle, Warren found absolutely nothing noteworthy about what impressed him as a rundown former Elks club building. Yet as Dave took him to every room (it was a short tour), he beamed with excitement about the many ways in which he believes God will use the church to impact the world.

Living in a valley where 150,000 people are scattered among numerous small townships, Dave has followed a multisite route of one church in many locations as his strategy for having an impact on his community and the world, a strategy that is profiled in two different books.[29]

The gist of his approach is to make it both simple and replicable. "We're not so much about multiplying campuses as about multiplying leaders," he told me. "When you multiply leaders, you need more places for them to lead, and therefore more campuses."[30] In most cases he encourages leaders to follow a simple progression: start a small group, start two or more small groups, and convene those groups as a worship center. That's it. In fact, the situation sounds a little like the hard-charging leaders of the frontier days!

This process has happened literally hundreds of times since Dave founded Christ the King Community Church in 1999 with 134 people in the first service. By the end of the church's first year, thirty-eight small groups were convening weekly in Jesus' name for Bible study, prayer, friendship, support, encouragement, and outreach. The church launched new worship centers in 2000 (two), 2001 (one), 2002 (one), 2003 (five), 2004 (five), and 2005 (four). So by the end of 2005, Christ the King was sponsoring locally twenty-six services on seventeen campuses, each in a different town, totaling 3,000 weekly worshipers. They are a dispersed megachurch trying to constantly send out more than they can afford.

As Warren explains in a profile he wrote elsewhere about Browning and the church, the Christ the King team surfaces leaders in a number of ways:

> Many leaders come to them, desiring to connect to the work that Christ the King is accomplishing. In other cases, Christ the King has placed simple ads in local newspapers, asking if readers were interested in being part of a new kind of church. The ads stated: "Are you an entrepreneurial Christian leader? Ready for a new kind of church in your area? Willing to be a strategic partner to make it happen? If your mission, vision and values intersect with

ours, then we're praying that you'll meet with us." The Christ the King team then meets with anyone who shows up at the designated meeting place (usually a public facility that they can use at no cost) and—voila!—the core group is established. A leader is identified, and through coaching, the team develops and then multiplies this initial group. When the number of groups reaches a certain critical mass, they begin a video worship experience, which eventually leads to the establishment of a regular weekend celebration.[31]

During 2005, Browning launched an Internet-based approach to training. It freed potential Christ the King site leaders from the need to be in geographical proximity to North Seattle. The number of empowered leaders, and thus the number of groups and worship sites, then began to multiply almost exponentially.

Fast-forward four years, when *Church Executive* magazine interviewed Dave Browning about the leaders he is empowering. The editor asked how many small groups there are at present. Browning replied, "That's a good question that I don't have a good answer for. It numbers in the thousands, and it has gotten out of control, which is okay by us." When the editor pressed him further, Browning figuratively acknowledged that he likes the problem: "Frankly, we are praying that this counting mess gets way worse, and that we will eventually have to throw up our hands in despair and say, 'We have absolutely no idea how many people are associated with our church.' That would be our dream." That kind of growth is what happens, he says, "when we put the ministry into the hands of people."[32]

We're not recommending chaos just for the sake of chaos, but we do find something compelling in Browning's model: his focus is on finding capable, teachable, Christ-like leaders who he can coach into new levels of church planting ministry. Christ the King is one more model of how aggressive local churches and church planting networks are leading the way in church planting at even greater levels than many denominations. As you decide to pursue a multiplying movement as your goal for life, it will cost a great deal. You will spend more time on it than you thought possible. But you will gain great joy from it as your multiplying church leads your faithful denomination to aggressively pursue God's redemptive plan.

5

KINGDOM COOPERATION

Church Planters Learning Together

Leadership Network Numbers

- **Cooperation Is Perhaps at an All-Time High**

  Today's generation of church planting organizations displays a heart of cooperation and sharing of resources. Free online tools abound—denomination training manuals, research papers, how-to articles, and audio and video training. This stems from a "kingdom mentality" in the church planting community that expands beyond denomination or regional allegiances.[1]

- **Larger Church Planting Centers Cross Denominational Lines**

  The more paid staff assigned to church planting for an organization, the more likely they were involved with other partners and providers, and the more churches they report having planted.[2]

- **Less Money Doesn't Decrease the Desire to Cooperate**

  National agencies are retooling to come alongside regional and local church planting efforts to provide help in recruiting, assessment, training, and coaching with lesser amounts of funding than in the past.[3]

Redeemer Presbyterian Church in New York City has become a multiplication center for other churches, and not just for those from its denomination, the Presbyterian Church in America. Since 1993, Redeemer has helped to plant over a hundred new churches—the majority of them non-Presbyterian. It has done so both directly and in partnership with other churches and denominations, such as the Southern Baptist Convention, Christian & Missionary Alliance, and Assemblies of God. Some of the new launches have been in greater New York City and others have been in such major global cities as Toronto, Amsterdam, Budapest, São Paulo, and Tokyo. Many of the planted churches have already given birth to churches of their own.

How has this happened? It is because Tim Keller, who in 1989 became founding pastor of Redeemer, believes passionately in the importance of church planting. "The only way to increase the number and percentage of Christians in a city is to plant thousands of new churches," he told Warren in an interview. Likewise, "the only way to change the culture in a city is to increase the number of churches engaged in it."

> *"The only way to increase the number and percentage of Christians in a city is to plant thousands of new churches."*
>
> —TIM KELLER

Redeemer has positioned itself as a church that wants to bless the city and do good to it—spiritually, socially, and culturally. Its mission statement brings out this idea, emphasizing church planting as a way to replicate and extend such influence. Redeemer's stated vision is "to spread the Gospel, first through ourselves and then through the city by word, deed, and community; to bring about personal changes, social healing, and cultural renewal *through a movement of churches* and ministries that change New York City and through it, the world (emphasis added).[4]

Redeemer started with a group of fifteen Christians meeting weekly for prayer. Their hope was that a new church could be opened in the heart of Manhattan to reach their friends, New Yorkers leading in various professions. Keller, who had been asked by his denomination to do field research on planting a church in New York City as he taught at Westminster Theological Seminary, built on that evangelistic heart when the embryo church launched its weekend services. "I asked them to tell me about their friends, and I'd preach in a way that would connect with them," he explained. "It was like a focus group, and my preaching changed quite a bit. I learned that if you preach as if non-Christians are there, Christians will bring their non-Christian friends to hear it. I also put them into leadership right away, and they built a church that would reach their friends."

By the church's fifth year, with attendance now exceeding one thousand, Redeemer planted its first two churches, one in lower Manhattan's Greenwich Village and another in the suburbs, both as Presbyterian Church in America congregations. "New churches best reach new generations, new residents, and new people groups," says Keller.

Was it hard for Redeemer as a young church to release people and money into these new works? Keller says:

> The congregation already owned the vision so it was not a big curve or surprise. . . . Interestingly, within a few weeks of sending off more than 100 people to start the two new congregations, our attendance regained what it lost. More interesting was the financial impact. For one of the new churches we asked the families we were sending to estimate how much they'd be giving financially the first year. [The projected total] was a sizeable amount. My first response was, "I bet they weren't giving us that kind of money!" But then I realized that's the genius of church planting: the new church was closer to their homes, and they dug deeper to help reach their community. That experience re-energized me. After that, our rhetoric spoke of church planting as "routine" for people to grow as disciples.[5]

Even though Redeemer continued to plant churches, Keller knew that one church's efforts—no matter how many new churches it started—would not be enough to reach New York City. "It's unreasonable and unworkable to have one single church planting movement here in New York," he says. So the year 2000 saw the formation of the Redeemer Church Planting Center. In less than a decade, it has become known as one of the nation's leading entities for kingdom cooperation for the purpose of church multiplication movements. The Redeemer Church Planting Center provides resources, including financing, mentoring, leadership, and ministers for church plants by Redeemer and by many other churches and denominations. Its purpose is to fuel and build a network of city, regional, national, and international church planting movements. Each is to be indigenous and contextualized to its city and culture within the framework of Redeemer's values of Gospel-centered and city-affirming ministry.

By expanding their vision toward New York City, the church has exponentially expanded its vision for the world. Redeemer Presbyterian Church and its planting center are an excellent model for showing how a drive for local kingdom impact can become a global movement of multiplying churches.

Redeemer Presbyterian Church and its planting center are an excellent model for showing how a drive for local kingdom impact can become a global movement of multiplying churches.

Terry Gyger, former executive pastor of the church and director of the church planting center, believes the most valuable contribution of the center is the training it offers to prospective urban church planters. "Training is virtually non-existent in the church planters who come here," he says. The training they need comes both through classroom study and on-site coaching. It starts before a church launches and continues during its opening months.

When Ed spoke at the Redeemer Alliance for Church Planting, representing Redeemer's efforts around metro New York, he remembers being surprised at just how broad the church planting coalition was. He looked around the room and could see everyone from Presbyterians (worshipping quietly) to Pentecostals (worshipping, well, not as quietly) gathered to learn about church planting. It was a diverse group with a common mission—planting churches that transform New York City with the Gospel.

Although a highly qualified staff has been raised and funded to staff Redeemer's center, Keller is still involved through vision casting, fund-raising, and even group mentoring. For example, four young pastors who are on the verge of planting churches in the New York area spend an hour with Keller every month, going through a syllabus. That personal interaction is part of an over-all program described as "Redeemer Labs," which was launched to spread the church's vision through books, online downloads, curricula, and other media approaches. Because of his vision and God's work through him, Keller is having an impact on a new generation of leaders to carry out a kingdom endeavor—a church multiplication movement.

How does Redeemer measure success with its church planting? Keller offers three standards: "First, are the churches reproducing? We figure that among all our aligned churches, if in any given year 10 percent are planting, then that means the movement is double every seven years. Second, do they have the Gospel DNA—the balance of word and deed? Third, is the city around those churches improving and do the people sense that the churches are a boon to their neighborhood?"[6]

Perhaps this is a good place for you to pause and use the previous few pages as a mirror to study your own church. A rapid multiplication movement occurs because lives are being changed by the church's message as the Gospel is advancing. We would challenge you to ask a question of your church: "If our church closed today, would the community miss us?" Perhaps you could ask an even stronger question: "Because our church is here, how has the community changed to better reflect the kingdom of God?"

As the people of your church mature spiritually, as the lost are being saved, and as other churches are being started, then change will occur in your overall neighborhood. It is critical that you find like-minded leaders with whom to partner so that not only your neighborhood can be transformed, but theirs can as well.

Even as Redeemer has grown to be one of the larger-attendance churches in New York City, and Keller's book, *The Reason for God*,[7] hit the *New York Times* bestseller list in 2008, Keller continues to affirm the need to ignite a multidenominational effort to plant new churches, both in New York City, across North America and around the world. "The vigorous, continual planting of new congregations is the single most crucial strategy for the numerical growth of the Body of Christ in any city, and for the continual corporate renewal

> *"New church planting is the only way that we can be sure we are going to increase the number of believers in a city and one of the best ways to renew the whole Body of Christ."*
>
> —TIM KELLER

and revival of the existing churches in a city," he says. "New church planting is the only way that we can be sure we are going to increase the number of believers in a city and one of the best ways to renew the whole Body of Christ."[8]

Redeemer is a powerful example of cooperation in church planting, but such cooperation is not without challenge. Ed remembers sitting in the back of a meeting hall in New York City with Keller as they were both speakers at an urban church planting conference called Dwell. They discussed the irony of talking about mission and kingdom cooperation while convening in that particular meeting hall—it was once a church facility that, in the name of cooperation at the beginning of the last century, lost its biblical moorings and eventually closed.

Cooperating Without Compromise

"The evangelization of the world in this generation!" was the cry of the world's first interdenominational gathering to promote and strategize missions. The year was 1888, the location was Mt. Herman, Massachusetts, and the organizing group was called the Student Volunteer Movement—which initially drew 250 students from eighty-seven colleges. Over the years, it grew to involve tens of thousands of students and was a strong force in sending out hundreds of students as missionaries for several decades. It was one of the first cooperative efforts among denominations on a national level, and it proved to be successful in most ways.

A similar rally cry fueled another great gathering, but after its first decade or so the results were very different. In 1910, church leaders came together in Edinburgh, Scotland, under the same slogan: "The evangelization of the world in this generation." Leaders of most major denominations were present to discuss how they could work together to win the world to Christ. They assumed that everyone who loves missions must also love the Bible and be committed to it in a similar way. Initially that was true, so differences in doctrine, structure, and polity were intentionally set aside for the purpose of helping each other send out missionaries.

Unfortunately, the follow-up conferences ultimately steered a different direction. By 1928 the International Missionary Council, which had been founded because of the 1910 meeting, questioned the need for personal witness and increasingly focused on service. The 1938 International Missionary Council meeting questioned the need for conversion among devout followers of other faiths. Though much good has been accomplished through the International Missionary Council and its successors, the historic lesson for many is that missions without a doctrinal framework tend to lose the Gospel's transformational power. No mission organization has maintained its focus on the Gospel without a strong doctrinal foundation.

In church planting efforts, similar concerns are often raised: how can we support each other without sacrificing our distinctive beliefs and practices?

Types of Partnerships

Same Denomination

Partnerships are a key value in church planting and they occur in a variety of different ways. The most basic occurs within a denomination and its own entities, such as when several levels cooperate to meet a need. For instance, a Southern Baptist church planter in Fresno, California, might have a need for training, so a partnership might form between the Fresno Baptist Association, the California State Convention, and the Georgia-based North American Mission Board, all working together. The national agency could officially commission the planter and family as missionaries and provide demographic information and high-altitude training. The state convention would then provide in-depth training on the mechanics of planting a church in the particular state. The local association provides a network for planters to gain encouragement and constant accountability. Without these partnerships, confusion and potential overlap often occur. These cooperative organizations recognize that people in the field are better suited to see the need for a church than a denominational state office located a hundred miles away, or a national office located a thousand miles away.

Intradenominational

The next type of partnership is typically called a network. Intradenominational networks operate as a specialized organization to assist churches by helping them partner together for best practices and best resources. They typically have common values and common pools of resources. Ultimately, however, they are built around a common (denominational) theology. The approach of many church planting centers today is to recognize that God's kingdom is made up of Presbyterians, Methodists, Baptist, Pentecostals, Lutherans, and others (this is hardly an exhaustive list). These groups maintain their distinctive doctrines while agreeing to a baseline orthodoxy. Yet they also work with each other by sharing such resources as knowledge and training. One predominantly intradenominational example is the NewThing network, profiled in Chapter Seven, many of whose churches are part of the restoration movement (the Christian Church emphasis of restoring the church of the New Testament rather than reforming the existing churches). Another intradenominational network is Seattle Church Planting, profiled later in this section.

Interdenominational

Interdenominational networks often form around a common paradigm of ministry or purpose. A good example is Redeemer Presbyterian's church planting network.

Local Church

A large number of networks emerge from the local church. For example, GlocalNet was birthed from NorthWood Church in Keller, Texas (this will be discussed further in Chapter Twelve). These networks are birthed out of the heart of the lead pastor, but the vision has been adopted by the entire congregation. Typically the lead pastor is a strong personality who uses the pulpit to frame the direction for the networks. Often each daughter church uses some variation of the name of the founding church.

Apostolic

Some churches, such as Ralph Moore's Hope Chapel that we profiled in Chapter Three, see themselves as apostolic. They look at every new believer and every emerging leader as a potential person to be sent out to start a new church. If these people remain connected to Hope Chapel, fine, but if not, fine. If they remain connected to the Foursquare denomination, fine, but if not, fine. Moore's heart is set on helping disciples grow, thus he seeks every possible opportunity to send them out to evangelize others and thereby populate the kingdom of God. (Be sure to read our earlier comments in Chapter Two about what we mean, and do not mean, by the term *apostolic*.)

However, too many churches call themselves apostolic, even referring to their main pastor as an apostle, but in reality they're doing little more than bringing existing churches into their corral. They want to provide an apostolic "covering" to other churches, but they often limit their approach to addition: churches sign up for their network, come to an annual conference, and hear good preaching designed to impart greater vision, inspire

Leaders who are at the forefront of multiplication movements are acting with an apostolic impulse because they live as someone sent by the kingdom and are busy sending others on behalf of the kingdom.

greater faith, and access greater spiritual passion. However, if it's based on the poor motive of bragging rights about the number of churches in their association then it has gone far afield from the New Testament record and the Greek term for apostle. In some cases, leaders who have the title "apostle" simply haven't really considered or seen other models of how to multiply their impact in a way that replicates leaders and truly advances God's kingdom. By contrast, leaders who are at the forefront of multiplication movements are acting with an apostolic impulse because they live as someone sent by the kingdom and are busy sending others on behalf of the kingdom. And—just to be clear—no title is necessary to do that.

For Many, Networks Are Eye-Opening

Church planting networks are a worldwide phenomenon. For example, leaders of the Antioch Movement in Ukraine still remember the day that denominational leaders in that country decided to trade their independent church planting efforts for a united approach of helping each other.

The fall of Communism ushered in religious freedom in the Ukraine and religious leaders began working together to assist each other in widespread church multiplication. "We tried to help churches understand that it is our country and we are responsible for it; it is our people and our churches who need to deliver and give birth to other churches," says a Ukrainian Christian leader who trains church planters in that country. "It is our God-given responsibility to bring the Gospel to each man, woman, and child and plant the churches. It is a huge vision."[9]

The culmination of the collaborative work of the Antioch Movement was when Baptist, Pentecostal, and independent church leaders came together to sign a historic plan in which each denomination's new churches added to the others would reach a combined total of twenty-eight thousand churches across Ukraine in their lifetime.

"They have pictures on their walls of the day where they signed the document," says Chad Smith of the Antioch Movement. "They had never sat together at the table before—this was the first step of seeing a movement in this nation."

Amazing things can happen when God's people find appropriate common ground and work together toward a dream that no one could accomplish alone.

How Networks Form

Networks form in as many different ways as there are people. Most start simply and practically. For example, Seattle Church Planting network began when Gary Irby, a Southern Baptist, tried to help start more new churches in the Southern Baptist tradition.

As a young minister in Washington state, Irby had served a church that was growing, albeit slowly. He had become frustrated with himself and with God. He said he prayed and did the things he needed to do to grow the church, but it just wasn't happening. So he asked God what the problem was. "God said to me very clearly—the clearest I've ever heard Him—'Gary, you've been adding. It's time to start multiplying.' In other words, God meant that it was my turn to get involved in church planting."

Irby has done just that. During his twenty years as a church planter—eleven of them in Seattle—Irby has been answering God's call to multiply. He's trained other church planters to do that as well. "A new church planter needs to start with the next one or two planters already on his team," Irby told us. "Partners need to bring a coalition of partners with them to the field, whether they need the help now or not. Even network and movement leaders must be reproducing themselves from day one."

Irby teaches his church planters to do likewise with those who support them through prayer and finances. They describe Partnership Development with four Ps as they find partners who will agree to

1. Pray (prayer support)
2. Play (mission involvement)
3. Pay (financial giving)
4. Parlay (be an advocate to bring along other partners)

Irby's office likewise is reproducing itself. Their Church Planting Administrative Hub has been a virtual office for church plants since 2004. This paid service currently administers fourteen of their church plants, helping with the clerical and administrative necessities of a new church. It's a good illustration of how church multiplication movements can uncover new ways to cooperate. It can be as simple as gathering all the planters in an area for prayer support, forming an administrative hub, getting multiple plants off the ground through funding, or sending some of the "won" people away to serve in other new churches. Multiplication comes with a joyful cost.

Gary Irby is also multiplying himself. Not in order to clone his personality behind new faces but to increase the capabilities of church planting in others. He has found the most painful part is to give away all types of ministry, especially the tasks he loves doing. Church planters have to make a similar change as their church plant grows. In the early stages, planters have a small band of core people with whom they spend significant time dreaming, eating, and living. As the church grows, the ability to invest time in those relationships lessens. To multiply yourself means giving others real opportunity, influence, and authority in ministry, as well as your time and attention in mentoring and training.

The same is true of a network that aspires to become a movement. Irby explains:

> When there were four or five church plants, I could spend signifi-
> cant time with each planter and his family, even playing the role of
> the occasional baby-sitter so the planting couple could have a date
> night. . . . As we've grown to over 80 new churches in our region,
> assisted in the planting of many more churches throughout the
> Northwest, and helped develop networks in many other partners
> of North America, that level of intimacy with each church plant-
> ing family is impossible to obtain. In order to grow to the next
> level, I must invest more and more time in those who invest in oth-
> ers who invest in the individual church planters and not as much
> in each church planter directly. For a highly relational, grace-giver
> such as myself, that is a difficult but necessary task.

Irby knows that a movement is not going to come from just one denomination or one network. "We must be intentional about initiating relationships and even partnerships with tribes other than our own," he observes. For example, he formed an ethnic church planting coalition in his region. "The group is currently comprised of the primary church planting leaders for about ten denominations/networks," he says. "This group is focused on helping each other to do a better job of planting within other cultures/ethnicities in our region. Together we represent about twenty-seven languages, yet we all have something to offer each other in significant ways. This has worked because our founding question was, 'What can we do together that we can't do apart if we don't care who gets the credit—other than God?'"

> *"Together we represent about twenty-seven languages, yet we all have something to offer each other in significant ways."*
>
> — Gary Irby

Pray, Dream, and Step Out—Please!

One of our hopes in writing this book is that more networks will form and that both new networks and existing networks will dream and trust God on a grander scale. We hope they dare to build a stronger element of multiplication in everything they do, pressing forward with greater confidence that what they are doing is wise and worthwhile.

We argued in Chapter Two that the Great Commission means to go plant evangelistic churches among all peoples, that the early church implemented the Great Commission mandate primarily by planting churches and that Paul's "missionary journeys" travels could be better called his "church planting journeys." This chapter has proposed that networks are an excellent vehicle for doing so, whether denominational, intradenominational, interdenominational, local-church based, or apostolic. Doing so probably means stepping beyond your comfort zone.

In fact, we church planting leaders often shy away from admitting that we have a comfort zone. As the "alpha dogs" of ministry, we hate thinking that anything could halt our forward motion. But there is a progression that we should observe:

Cooperation → Training → Delegation → Commission

In order to build networks that effectively lead, mentor, and support others in multiplication movements, everyone must pass what they know and what they do on to someone else. If you will begin to view cooperation as a joyful opportunity to cause someone else to succeed, then giving away all you have for the sake of a new or established network is worth the effort. Church multiplication movements will occur only so far as leaders are ready to cooperate for a cause that is far greater than themselves.

6

PREDICTORS OF SUCCESS

Recruitment, Assessment, and Deployment

Leadership Network Numbers

- **Assessment, Training, and Coaching Help Reach the Unchurched**

With few exceptions, those involved in church planting systems (assessment, basic training, and coaching) reach more unchurched people and grow more rapidly than those who are not.[1]

- **Assessment, Training, and Coaching Increase Church Survivability**

The increased success rate of church plants in the last decade is directly correlated to the advent of assessment, training, and coaching incorporated into national and regional strategies.[2]

- **Assessment Is Now the Norm**

Three-quarters (73 percent) of regional denomination agencies report that they have a formalized church planter assessment system in place.[3]

- **Training Systems Are Going Online**

Over half (53 percent) of denominational regions have a specific training system for church planting, and just under half (43 percent) of regions now have online training resources available.[4]

- **Internships Are Still the Minority**

Only 16 percent of regional initiatives provide church planter internships.[5]

Twenty years ago, to be a church planter meant one thing: you were alone in the universe. Church planting was embarked upon alone by the planter's family; a planter was viewed as an interloper by local pastors, and perceived as the nutcase who could not get a real ministry position by other churches. You were on your own.

Sometimes it worked and sometimes it didn't. When it fell apart, it hurt both the planters and the members of the plant. Everyone went away with scars, disillusionment, and pain. Quality people spent months and sometimes years on the sidelines, processing and healing from what was often an excruciating and perplexing experience.

Those who commissioned church planters went through a similar process. They had interviewed prospective church planters, they had prayed for discernment, they had helped identify a fertile location for the new church, and they had invested time and funds in the new work. When it went south, they too felt the hurt.

We've both planted churches in that way. Chapter Two tells a bit of Ed's story, as he and his wife tried virtually on their own to reach the urban poor in Buffalo. Warren planted a church under a national program with his denomination, but it was an approach that his local ministry supervisor openly disliked and criticized. A few weeks after Warren's church plant launched, the national church planting leader resigned—and Warren felt very alone.

Both of us felt the loneliness that accompanied church planting in those days. But even more, we felt unprepared. Perhaps the memories of those days has been what God has used to drive us to write, speak, and train people like crazy for the work of church planting.

But there was one place where we found refuge during the early days of our church planting work—the ministry of Bob Logan. Over the years Logan has been a long-distance mentor to both of us. We've read his books, listened to his audio recordings since the time when they were available on a now-extinct system of audios called cassette tapes, heard him at conferences, and interacted with him personally. He is someone who has been on both sides of the divide: he has planted churches with inadequate support and he has tried to resource church planters, but with feelings of inadequacy for lack of good tools to give them.

Logan strikes us as a systems guy who would have been an engineer if God hadn't called him to be a pastor. He is a visionary, so he would have designed great projects as an engineer.

So it's an unusual thing for a personality like Logan (who was the son of an engineer) to say that God sent him a dream in 1977 when he was a young church planter. But it represents a turning point in his ministry and is a story he repeats often. As he was a struggling church planter, he cried out to God for help. And God surprised Logan with a vision—something outside of his theological grid at the time. The gist of his vision is that he's on the beach of his native California and he sees a crowd of church planters numbering in the thousands. God spoke to them in a loud voice: "Okay, everyone, listen up! Your objective is to swim to Catalina Island, twenty-two miles away." The starting pistol fired and the planters entered the water. They obediently began to swim. Some began to cramp up. Some sank immediately. Many were done in by the tricky currents. Only a few made it.

As church planter after church planter was pulled into the same undercurrent, making the same fatal mistakes over and over, Logan began asking God questions: "Why aren't there buoys to warn them of hazards to avoid during the swim? Why aren't there lifeboats to rescue those who are going under? Why aren't the church planters who have completed the swim successfully returning to show others how to do it? Lord, we're not learning from the successes or failures of other church planters. This isn't right! I promise you this: If you ever place me in the position to help the others who are lined up on the shore, that's what I want to do. I will give my life to provide resources to help leaders be more fruitful in making disciples."

For Bob Logan, this was a dream of multiplication. "2 Timothy 2:2 has had a profound impact on me," he says, "showing me that leadership development is the limiting factor in most churches."

> "In the church multiplication movements now forming, most of the leaders of the future churches are not yet Christians."
>
> —BOB LOGAN

The verse shows four generations: "What you have heard from me in the presence of many witnesses, commit to faithful men who will be able to teach others also." To Logan, the fourth generation is when multiplication begins to show fruit, revealing your true DNA. Likewise, he says, "churches shouldn't claim they've multiplied successfully until they have birthed great-grandchildren." That means, he says, that "in the church multiplication movements now forming, most of the leaders of the future churches are not yet Christians." It is a thought that simultaneously makes your brain hurt to think about and your heart burn to consider its implications.

Several decades later, Logan continues to live out that calling. His extensive training and coaching materials are among the finest available, (see www.coachnet.org). On a personal level, since 2007 he has returned to hands-on church planting work, cultivating a network of ethnic leaders who are starting and multiplying house churches. Named ViaCordis (Latin for "way of the heart"), its leaders all serve bivocationally.

Approaches to Training

Aristotle has been quoted as saying, "Excellence is an art won by training and habituation. We do not act rightly because we have virtue or excellence, but we rather have those because we have acted rightly. We are what we repeatedly do. Excellence, then, is not an act but a habit." If we are to see church multiplication movements ramp up in North America and continue their increase in the rest of the world, then "training and habituation" are nonnegotiables for church planters.

Today a growing number of churches in our country desire to advance the kingdom of God through the multiplication of new churches. Many of these churches are catching a vision for starting multiple churches every year, churches that will then in turn reproduce aggressively. Fortunately, these church planting churches see the necessity for training of their church planters. They see training as foundational to the success of a new church. However, they use a wide variety of models, all designed to address critical issues in an intentional manner. Following are the five leading leadership models in use.[6]

Boot Camp

One of the most popular ways that churches train church planting leaders is an intensive approach, often referred to as a boot camp. This is a concentrated, intensive training experience that lasts two to four days.

In the intensive Church Planter's Training Program designed by Bob Logan, for example, church planting leaders invest a significant amount of time prior to the week of training.[7] In their preparation for training, they work through multiple worksheets and exercises. Doing so is absolutely essential because the training experience itself is built around focusing and refining through personal coaching. The preparation has two primary objectives: (1) to provide the leaders with an opportunity for prayerful reflection and personal discussions about the specific church they anticipate starting, and (2) to prepare leaders to apply their reflections in the boot camp when coaches will be present to help. The entire process is organized around five personal operating questions:

- Who am I?
- What am I called to do?
- Who will do it with me?
- How will we do it?
- How will we evaluate our progress?

Participants learn not by teachers presenting to them so much as by discovery. Bob Logan says, "The great teachers of the past—Jesus as the best example—have always used discovery learning principles."

Turbo Training

Another variety of an intensive approach is nicknamed turbo training. This is a concentrated two-day experience where church planting leaders receive a substantial amount of content, interspersed with small-group process and interaction. This information-rich approach to training, like drinking water from a fire hose, might hurt a little but certainly fills you up fast. This system is designed to help leaders understand the "essential questions" that they must wrestle with in their development process.

The two-day turbo training is followed—typically a month later—with a third day of training focused on making missional disciples and leaders in a new church. The strength of this system is its emphasis on a missional ecclesiology. It defines missional as acting and behaving like a missionary. Thus the church community both sees itself and functions just as if it

> *It defines missional as acting and behaving like a missionary.*

was a missionary. We find that an overlooked yet inherent strength for many turbo trainings is the emphasis on quickly moving the information from planter to people. Hopefully, each type of training offered strives to do the same. This system challenges church planting leaders to think carefully and critically about what they are doing.

Content Driven

One of the groups that uses a more content-driven boot camp approach is called the Acts 29 Network, a transdenominational network that seeks to perpetuate the church planting passion seen in the twenty-eight chapters of the book of Acts.

The Acts 29 Network was cofounded by Mark Driscoll and David Nicholas. Founding pastor of Mars Hill Church in Seattle, Washington. Mark Driscoll, has become an extremely popular teacher and leader among younger pastors in America. He is Acts 29's best-known leader. Much of the drive for strong, purposeful content has its genesis with Driscoll, whose Sunday messages regularly exceed one hour during worship services.

The Acts 29 Boot Camp places a strong emphasis on Reformed Theology, male eldership, and contextualizing the Gospel for current culture. They offer such training several times each year (and Ed frequently teaches missiology and church planting in those gatherings). Though nothing can replace the experience of personally attending a training event, Acts 29 is also a leading purveyor of training content on the Internet and holds a strong publishing presence, thanks to their emphasis on driving good content to potential planters and those already in the field.

Leadership is a topic that is spoken of in seminary, but cannot truly be learned until a person has experienced the opportunity to actually lead something. This is also true of church planting and amplified if one is hoping to lead a multiplication movement. Boot camps, whether turbo training or content-driven events, offer church multiplication movement leaders insights that could otherwise take years to gain on their own. We suggest that in your quest to lead a movement that you take a few days from your life to hear from some mentors who are already further down the journey.

Training Classes

Although the majority of church-planting churches follow the boot camp model of intensive training, some believe that training needs to be spread out over several weeks or several months in order for there to be better assimilation and integration of learning. West Ridge Church in Atlanta, Georgia is one example. Jim Akins, the church planting director at West Ridge, says, "I prefer to stretch out the training over five months. We meet one Saturday every month for the entire day." According to Akins, "Planters don't have time to process their learning when it comes too fast. They don't know what to do with it."

Akins and his senior pastor, Brian Bloye, use a compilation of *Essentials for Starting a Missional Church*, Bob Logan's *Church Planter's Toolkit*, and *The North American Mission Board (NAMB) Basic Training*, spreading out the content of the curriculum over many months. Each month the planters in training receive assignments to complete. At the monthly meetings they report on how they are applying previous learning. This is sometimes done in written form but usually it is done orally within the group. Then they discuss something new that was learned from that month's experience. Finally, they share something that they have come to realize they need in their personal development. An unseen benefit to this process is the development of an unofficial network between planters. Members of training classes often develop a sense of camaraderie that outlives the time spent in training. Something about learning together makes for strong bonds among church planters.

During these months, the planters in training are exposed to key staff and former church planters from West Ridge. They all share personal stories and give examples of some of their best practices. Akins says, "I want our planters in training to see both theory and practice." He expects his trainees to begin the planting process before the nine months are completed.

Another church that uses a training class approach is Redeemer Presbyterian Church in New York City, which was introduced in the previous chapter. At Redeemer's church planting center, however, they prefer to limit their training to planters who are actively planting in the city. Redeemer's Mark Reynolds prefers "just in time" training that is presented in a sequential process over nine to twelve months. He believes that this is important to enable the planters to absorb the material. At Redeemer, each instructional unit contains three phases: preparation and enrichment (for example, homework, reading, assignments, and the like), instruction (class room sessions), and practice (applying and doing what one is learning in a live planting context). The training program consists of ten monthly sessions and typically enrolls ten to eighteen New York planters.

Whereas boot camps focus on preparatory learning, training classes focus on "real time" training. Both have their place in the development of leaders for church multiplying. Boot camps get you started and training classes can keep you going.

Internship or Apprenticeship

Some church planting churches prefer to have their trainees on site for an extended period of time so that the trainees can experience the culture of the mother church while receiving practical experience. This approach is typically referred to as an internship or apprenticeship approach. Church networks that follow this approach work with as many as a dozen high-potential church planting interns per year. The group typically meets weekly for assignments, debriefings, and discussion. It may also engage in an online learning community process to help them learn from one another's experiences. The idea is for the interns to have experience actually doing most of the things that a church planter must do to succeed. The process may last six to twelve months.

Crosspointe Church in Orlando, Florida, illustrates this approach. Chan Kilgore, the lead pastor, has created a one-year apprenticeship for high potential church planting prospects. In this year-long process, apprentices also participate in intensive training events such as the Acts 29 Boot Camp. Much attention and accountability is also built around developing spiritual disciplines, establishing a strong theological basis for church planting, and cultivating a strong missiology. "It's very important that our planters know the Gospel well and be able to connect the story of the Gospel with the story of people's lives," states Kilgore. "Plus, I have them set goals for each trimester for personal and missional development."

The strength of an internship or apprenticeship approach is the ongoing, personalized mentoring given to the prospective planter. There is also the opportunity to learn within a dynamic, thriving church environment. However, most interns and apprentices have to find ways to support themselves financially during the process. This is usually accomplished through a spouse's income, raising support, outside employment, or a combination of these.

Residency Approach

An approach that appears to be growing in popularity is the residency approach. This is very similar to the internship or apprenticeship approach, but in a residency the trainees generally receive a full-time salary and are treated more as an extension of the mother church's professional staff. As a result, most residency churches have one or just a few residents. A residency for a planter is true on-the-job training.

A residency for a planter is true on-the-job training.

Perimeter Church in greater Atlanta is one example of a congregation offering a church planting residency. Perimeter's residency is a two-year program. They target seminary graduates and young pastors who want to pursue church planting. In the first year the focus is on training within Perimeter whereas the second year is devoted to actual work "in the field," assisting another church planter. The training currently revolves around three priorities: (1) Perimeter's best practices; (2) ongoing experiences at teaching and doing ministry; and (3) young church planting observation and experience.

Perimeter encourages their residents to participate in other training events. During the last six months of the two-year residency, residents step out and begin actually doing the work to prepare for their new church.

Hill Country Bible Church in Austin, Texas, has one of the largest church planting residency programs in the country. Though they hope all their residents will plant a new church, one does not have to be totally committed to that direction before entering the program at Hill Country. "Residency helps to prove out that they are ready to plant," states Craig Foster, an elder at Hill Country. "The goal is to learn through experience more than formal training." This residency lasts for twelve months, in the hopes that it will guide residents into church planting. If so, then six additional months are devoted to prelaunch preparation. Predictably there are a high number of applicants for only a few slots.

For Hill Country, the key to the residency is mentoring. Each year there are four new residents, with two being mentored by staff while two are being mentored by lay leaders in the church.

As part of the training, residents and their families must visit the other church plants in the association and complete an evaluation form about the church's development in relation to various criteria given.

A church planting residency can be a deeply enriching experience for prospective church planters. It gives many prospective planters an excellent opportunity to explore, research, and learn as they prepare for their own church planting venture. Like internships, the personalized mentoring and the opportunity to learn within a dynamic, thriving church environment are great advantages. However, for most churches, a residency program represents a significant financial commitment. Because of this, very few churches are able to support more than one or two at a time.

Churches like Perimeter and Hill Country have decided to focus on residencies. They are investing a massive amount of resources in residencies in order to help launch multiplication movements. We believe residency training can help keep a potential planter moving from learning to launching to multiplying. We hope that more churches will choose to do the same.

Informal Training

Church of the Highlands in Lakeland, Florida, takes an informal approach to training—one the church began when it was less than a year old. The team there believes that training best happens through informal mentoring and training. Hal Haller, the founding pastor of Church of the Highlands (which is now planting churches up and down the Interstate 4 corridor), says that he invites guys to just "hang out with me." That's what Ricc Conner did.

Conner was a student pastor in another church when he began to sense God's call to plant a church. Not sure of how to best proceed, he accepted Haller's invitation to hang out with the team at Church of the Highlands. He raised some support and secured some additional part-time work to support himself. He then sold his home and moved to the ministry area to begin his work with Hal. The training at Church of the Highlands is not formal or structured. People like Conner simply come and hang out for about six months, during which time they are given some responsibilities, some short-term tasks, and lots of time with senior leaders in the church. "You get involved in all the ministries, greeting, ushering, children, drama, you name it," says Conner. Theirs is a Paul-Timothy model of training.

Typically, each prospective planter will demonstrate the ability to effectively start a small group before any funding is considered for their church plant down the road. Trainees gather groups at places like Starbucks to prove that they can gather a following. All the planters find ways to support themselves so as not to be a burden to the church. This enables the church to have numerous prospective planters engaged in this informal training at once.

Here, the advantage we see in respect to a multiplication movement is that informal training can reveal the abilities of a person's natural charisma. As the vision for such movements spreads throughout our established church planting culture of addition, more and more planters (and potential planters) will need to move into friendships with movement leaders to see what all the fuss is about. For many out there, they have the skills, personality, and determination to spearhead a movement but they need a personal friendship with a leader to draw it out of them. To the leaders, we say, "Find a Timothy." To the hopeful planters, we say, "Find a Paul."

Assessment at the Front

The five types of training systems described in the preceding section have various levels of formality. All are somewhat entrepreneurial. Some are highly flexible, able to expand and handle many more church planters, should the opportunity arise. Others, particularly those heavily funded by a sponsoring church or outside donors, have a higher degree of accountability. All are designed to help multiple church planters to start multiple churches.

Whatever the approach, most training systems incorporate an assessment process, an interview-based approach to helping prospective church planters answer, "Is this God's call on my life?" Why? Because a lot of people who shouldn't plant a church try to. We've met some of them. They are upset that their church won't let them preach, so they start a blog about everything wrong with the church. They write it from their bedroom in mom's basement as they sit in their beds with Star Wars sheets and covers. Then they decide to show the world how it should be done, but the result is a train wreck. Hence, we need assessments!

The most widely used one was developed by Dr. Charles Ridley, a professor and licensed psychologist. He was approached by Carl George, long-time director of the Charles E. Fuller Institute of Evangelism and Church Growth, who organized a group of denominations to find out how to better screen church planter candidates. Ridley's study brought together a group of successful and unsuccessful church planters, so as to understand the full range of performance characteristics. The study may be limited due to the fact that those studied were primarily Anglo North Americans. Ridley, an African-American, described in the process that for the majority of the North American population the assessment would be accurate. He came up with a long list of common characteristics that he then narrowed down to thirteen. It should be noted, however, that this approach has been adopted in other cultures and countries as well.

Eventually, the six most critical characteristics came to be known as the "knock-out" categories. Ridley developed a four-hour behavioral interview where a trained assessor meets with an interested church planter candidate and asks a series of questions. These questions enable the assessor to ferret out of the candidate the information indicating whether or not they possess certain behaviors. Theological evaluations and reference checks are necessary, but the assessment is not about those issues. Instead, theological criteria and background criteria are left to the discretion of churches, denominations, and networks based on their unique makeup.

Ridley's assessment is a behavioral assessment tool that helps the interviewer know how this individual is wired. For instance, if you're going to be the starter of a new church then you definitely need to demonstrate a history of starting things (religious, secular, business, and so on). As assessors look at these characteristics, they can discover who could be most effective in church planting.

The benefits of an assessment process are many. They give the potential church starter an opportunity to examine themselves, with trained persons helping them to see their strengths and limitations. The process might enable a potential church starter to improve abilities and correct limitations.

Assessment can help identify the type of church starting effort that "fits" the potential church planter. Finally, it may also avert a potential disaster. Though everyone can help plant a church, not everyone is wired to be a church planter. Assessment helps those who do not have a call or giftedness for church planting to focus on areas of ministry where

> *Though everyone can help plant a church, not everyone is wired to be a church planter.*

there is a proper fit. Sadly, we have observed both the sudden implosion and the slow, painful deaths of church plants in the lives of friends about whom we cared deeply. It was hard to watch as outsiders, and certainly these were excruciating experiences to live through. We believe that honest assessments done in the spirit of Christian friendship can help some well-meaning people to avoid planting and find their proper role the church.

There are several components to an effective assessment process. These typically include a self-assessment, an assessment interview or, for some, an assessment connected with an internship.

Any personal assessment process is difficult. People tend to take the assessment personally and feelings can get hurt. They have to understand that they may be extremely gifted to be a great pastor, but perhaps not a church planter. Even so, the process can lead people to feel as if they are being judged, and obviously sometimes the assessors make the wrong decisions. But the point is to save well-intentioned persons from failing at what they are not qualified to do, and there are several levels of outcomes in an assessment process:

- You may be assessed as qualified and ready to start planting a church immediately.

- You may be helped to discover that you do not possess the qualities that are needed to do this, and be redirected into other ministry options.

- You may learn that you have some of the necessary experience, maturity, or training, but that these are not yet sufficiently developed to begin planting immediately.

- Related to the previous point, you may find that an internship served under a trained mentor will help supply the specific qualifications needed.

We find that honest assessment, though difficult to hear, can be extremely freeing. Often, assessors are able to articulate what the planter, his spouse, and those around already knew. With that affirmation, would-be planters can find the ministry that God has for them.

A Wide Variety of Fanatics

With this chapter, we have looked at how recruitment, assessment, and deployment can benefit the planter. But please do not miss a universal message inherent in the chapter—it takes all types of training to recruit all types of planters so the world can have all types of churches in order to reach all types of people. A one-size-fits-all approach is naive at best and callous at worst. Church multiplication movements value the variety of ways in which the overall church is assaulting the gates of hell. We hope that every kind

It takes all types of training to recruit all types of planters so the world can have all types of churches in order to reach all types of people.

of biblically faithful congregation in existence will take up the cause to find a way—perhaps every way—they can imagine to call out, train up, and send off an army of church planting fanatics.

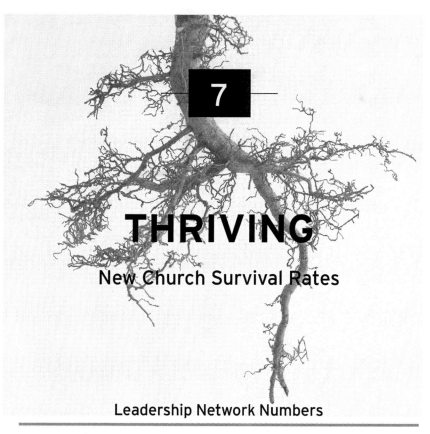

7

THRIVING

New Church Survival Rates

Leadership Network Numbers

- **Most New Churches Survive**

Two years after being started, 92 percent of new churches still exist. After three years, 81 percent still exist. After four years, 68 percent still exist.[1]

- **Average Attendance Is Eighty-four in a New Church's Fourth Year**

At the one-year mark, average attendance of a new church is forty-one people. At the two-year mark, it's fifty-six. At the three-year mark, it's seventy-three. At the four-year mark, it's eighty-four.[2]

- **Three of Ten New Churches Become Self-Sufficient in Year One**

A full 30 percent of new churches attain self-sufficiency in the first year, 40 percent in the second, 54 percent in year three, 62 percent in year four, and 70 percent attain it by year five. It is a long-held principle that churches must become self-sufficient in order to have long-term survivability.[3]

- **Up-Front Funding and Staffing Do Make a Difference**

Church plants that grow larger faster tend to be more heavily resourced and staffed than those that do not.

W hat do you do if you find that your sibling has the same drive to plant a church as you? Dive headlong into the work with abandon and use the natural sparks that fly in such a relationship to drive it beyond your wildest dreams. At least that what the Fergusons did.

Ever since Dave Ferguson, younger brother Jon Ferguson, and three of their college buddies planted Community Christian Church, Naperville, Illinois, in 1989, they have been working hard to give everything away—the church's people, its money, its talent, and in many ways, themselves. This is something they want to do continually, not just as a one-time effort.

Every person who is part of Community Christian, from volunteer leader to pastor, is continually training up new leaders to replace themselves. From the worship arts to small groups, the church's DNA is one of reproduction, always with the church's mission in mind of helping as many people as possible to "find their way back to God."

In addition, Community Christian has also reproduced itself through their number of locations. They went multisite in 1998, developing eleven Chicago-area locations by 2010. They have also reproduced themselves by setting up a network of affiliate churches that they've helped plant twenty-five churches in their first eight years.

They call their network of interdenominational churches NewThing, taken from the "new thing" that God is doing among his people, according to Isaiah 43:19 (NIV). NewThing's mission is "to be a catalyst for a movement of reproducing churches." That's quite an undertaking! But it is a vision that will serve as a catalyst in their movement and as a spark for other movements.

NewThing participants, under the leadership of Jon Ferguson, take this mission very seriously. Churches in the network must agree to what Ferguson calls "four crucial components" as depicted in the following box.

NewThing Network Accountability Structure for Reproduction

1. *Leadership Development Process for Individual Leaders and Artists*

Principle: The responsibility of developing leaders is shared by every leader in the church.

Specific Measures: The process for developing individual leaders may vary from church to church depending on creativity or context, but the principles of every leader intentionally developing other leaders formally and relationally is a constant in every reproducing church.

- Apprentice model implemented in every department or ministry
- Coaching model applied in every department or ministry
- Leadership Residents in the mix

2. *Leadership Development Program for the Entire Organization*

Principle: Leaders will be empowered and equipped by the church.

- **Specific Measures:** A formal, regular gathering of all leaders and apprentice leaders from every ministry that includes a combination of:
- Vision: What are we about? Where are we going?
- Huddle: How does this play out in my particular area of ministry?
- Skill: How do we do it? What do we need to learn?

3. *Metrics in Place to Measure All Aspects of Reproduction*

Principle: Measure what matters. Without constant visual measurement, leadership development processes and programs become wishful thinking.

Specific Measures: A dashboard tool is in place that measures how many leaders are being developed through the regular program (for example, Leadership Community) and how effectively they are being developed. A reproducing goal is put before leadership as a next step.

4. A Commitment to Church Reproduction

Principle: Put your resources where your values are.
Specific Measures: A clear goal and action plan for launching a new campus or a new church.

- Leadership Residents in training
- Reproduction funds as part of the church's general operations budget

Churches Can Truly Multiply Like Crazy

"Only 20 percent of all church plants survive." This statistic gets thrown around a lot in church planting circles by successful plant-ers rejoicing that they have overcome the odds, by frustrated church planters looking to justify their failures, and by territorial leaders of existing churches hoping to discourage potential com-petition for people and resources. The statistic is staggering—or would be if it were true. As we outlined earlier in the Leadership Network Numbers, 92 percent of new churches make it to their second anniversary. Four years after launching, 68 percent of church plants still exist.

Unfortunately, the "Chicken Little" syndrome has run rampant in the church planting world. The inaccurate 20 percent statistic hinders work toward multiplication by causing leaders to develop tunnel vision. Against these "overwhelming" odds, survival, not multiplication, becomes the goal. Vital steps toward multiplica-tion are put off "until we're ready." For a church planter to become ready to plant a network of churches is like a young married couple preparing to start their family of children. You can prepare a little, but eventually you have to take a leap of faith. Don't allow rumors and false statistics to get in the way of your obedience.

NewThing became a reality in 2001 when Dave Richa left his role as student ministry director at Community Christian to plant a church in the Denver, Colorado area. He took thirty-five people from Community Christian with him. Both churches wanted to stay closely connected with each other, with both featuring the same "Big Idea" each week and working collaboratively to develop it. (The "Big Idea" is a strategy to focus all teaching and programming, at all age levels, on one specific theme each week. The Fergusons, along with Creative Arts Director Eric Bramlett, wrote a book to explain it.[4]) Focusing on a like-minded strategy within a network can be counted as a contributing factor for new church survivability.

The churches figured out an inexpensive way to video-conference together each week. As Community Christian planted other churches, they too joined the weekly video-conference. Over time everyone realized that they weren't merely sharing content for their sermons, children's programming and the like; they were reproducing church culture in each other.

As the number of NewThing's participating churches increased, it was harder for the Fergusons to connect relationally with each church planter, even with an annual face-to-face meeting of all the lead pastors. The next big step for NewThing was to expand from one network to three network hubs. This was a huge step because no longer were the vision and the push to reproduce coming from one central location.

At the 2008 lead pastor gathering, the number of network hubs went from three to six. As of 2010, NewThing has over fifty churches or sites, six networks, and a target of doubling the number of churches and sites each year. Reproduction breeds life. For church planting, multiplication

Reproduction breeds life. For church planting, multiplication provides viability.

provides viability. If you want your church to live, the produce more leaders than you think you will ever need.

Jon Ferguson's focus has been to keep simplifying the process. "We will see a movement of multiplying churches only when we simplify," he told us. "Most of our systems are way too complex. They require too much time and too much money; too many buildings and too many professionals." Simplification is a trend returning to American church methodology in the early twenty-first century. During our formative years in the ministry, it was stressed to us that you need a multitude of programs ready to go at the launch of your church. Now even long-established churches are looking for ways to scale back the internal weight that accompanies an overload of programming. Stagnation of growth often follows closely on the heels of bloated church programming. Explosive growth often follows easily reproducible ministries.

Yet, even with constant simplification, leaders at Community Christian Church have had to also increase their flexibility. "I've had to get increasingly more comfortable with the messiness of multiplication," Jon Ferguson says. "It's not safe, predictable, or manageable. It's risky, spontaneous, and seemingly out of control." To our church planting hearts, this sounds like fun!

The success to date is not seen only in the growth of the NewThing network. An even more encouraging sign comes from what the church planters request. "We are creating a dashboard to count some of the important statistics and for some healthy accountability which will be extremely helpful to meeting our goals," says Jon. "We keep hearing over and over from the lead pastors that this is what they need—more accountability to reproduce."

Factors Influencing Survivability

NewThing, along with the dozens of other church planting networks, represent a tremendous step forward in helping new churches both survive and thrive. It's a quantum leap between holding one prayer meeting for church planters and then sending them off into the sunset.

We recognize that it is essential that people be given permission to plant churches. We have talked about that extensively elsewhere in this book. But what about when churches, networks or denominations plant churches like NewThing? We have found that this effort requires systems to increase survivability.

These newer models of peer networking, coaching, shared resources, and so on, are fortunately widespread enough that we can survey new churches to find out which of them influence survivability and health. Ed did a big research project for the North American Mission Board in which a team that he oversaw conducted exactly five hundred telephone-interview surveys among new churches from twelve evangelical denominations. Based on those interviews, over a hundred factors were tested. A handful indicated a statistically significant relationship to survivability. Thanks to the North American Mission Board, which granted us permission to do so, we included these numbers in the larger Leadership Network report, which is reflected in the "Leadership Network Numbers" cited at the beginning of this chapter. They show that the failure rate of new churches is much lower than common stereotypes: one-third were self-supporting, one-third were still a mission, and one-third had ceased to exist.[5]

Realistic Expectations Increase Survivability

The likelihood of survivability increases by over 400 percent when the church planter has a "realistic" understanding and expectations of the church planting experience. We know that "realistic" is a painfully subjective term. But all planters must tie their expectations to who they are and where they plant. They must base their expectations in the tangible world of their own skills, the limitations inherent in their church model, and the demographic probabilities of their community.

However, before you say we are nothing more than shallow pragmatists, we want to affirm that God can do more with the unexpected person than with the star quarterback who is bankrolled by a megachurch and has a solid pedigree. Yes, God often chooses the "Gideon" to win the battle. All we can say from observation is that successful church planters begin their plant with a realistic view that they will not be the size of a mega-reproducing network until they have paid the proper price to get there.

Church Members Welcome Leadership Development

The likelihood of church survivability increases by over 250 percent when the church offers leadership development training to new church members. As you have seen from the illustrations in this chapter and throughout the book, the DNA of a church plant is critical for the launching of a multiplication movement. Leaders must be developed early and often in a plant. One of the great lessons for planters is to learn how to delegate work without abandoning the new leader. Instead, bring new leaders along to build faith and skill before launching them into their assignment.

Stewardship Plans Are Helpful

The likelihood of church survivability increases by 178 percent when there is a proactive stewardship development plan within the church plant designed to help it become financially self-sufficient.

It Helps to Have a Church Planter Peer Group

The likelihood of church survivability increases by 135 percent when the church planter meets at least monthly with a group of church planting peers. If you are a planter or even a movement leader, then admit it—you have an alpha mentality. You naturally take control and lead the conversation, plan the next event, and generally take over every party you attend. You're usually busy leading, so you're probably not used to hanging around with peers. Regularly meeting with a group of fellow church planters will provide you spiritual protection, accountability, and an awareness of what God is doing in and through other churches. Peer groups are helpful because they keep a planter focused on the larger picture of God's kingdom instead of on the planter's own smaller picture. You would do well to be reminded on a regular basis that your thing isn't the only thing God has going.

What Makes Plants Excel

We've identified what helps a new church survive, but mere survival isn't the goal. We want to see churches that excel. The declining state of church attendance in North America has a tendency to lower our standards for celebration. These days many applaud growth of any kind and at any cost. We'd like to suggest shooting for a greater goal. We are encouraged by positive growth in any church, no matter the size. But let's not be naive. All of us should settle for nothing less than a Pentecost event. We should strive for an Acts 2 type of growth where thousands stand in rapt attention at the power of the Gospel and beg to be part of the church, where unbelievers long to know how they can have what believers have in Jesus Christ. But that's a hard matter to survey across many denominations and across the wide variety of ways new churches start. But because we're researchers, we are always ready to give it a shot. Following are the findings on two basic areas.[6]

Many Factors Relate to Growth

In reviewing the combined four-year mean attendance of church plants, a number of factors were found to be associated with higher attendance:

- Meeting in a school in the first year over not meeting in a school in the first year

- Meeting in a theater in subsequent years over not meeting in a theater in subsequent years
- Meeting in a school in subsequent years over not meeting in a school in subsequent years
- Conducting a special children's event (such as a fall festival, Easter egg hunt)
- Mailing invitations to services, programs, events
- Conducting new member classes
- Using a church covenant signed by new members
- Starting at least one daughter church within three years of the church plant
- Having a proactive stewardship development plan enabling the church to be financially self-sufficient
- Having multiple staff members rather than a single staff member at the beginning of the church plant
- Being financially compensated as the church planter
- Receiving health insurance whereby the majority of the premiums were paid for by the church plant, sponsoring church, or denomination
- Conducting a block party as an outreach event
- Delegating leadership roles to church members
- Conducting leadership training to church members
- Working full-time over part-time as the church planter
- Being assessed prior to planting the church as the church planter

Many of these factors are touched upon in other chapters of this book. Or, if you find one that is not mentioned in this book, it will certainly be found in some of the resources in the bibliography.

Many Factors Relate to Baptism or Conversion

In reviewing the combined four-year mean attendance of church plants, the following factors were found to be associated with higher baptism counts:

- Engaging in ministry evangelism (for example, food banks, shelters, drug and alcohol recovery programs)
- Starting at least one daughter church within three years of the church plant
- Having a proactive stewardship development plan enabling the church to be financially self-sufficient
- Conducting a midweek children's program
- Conducting a children's special event (such as a fall festival, Easter egg hunt)
- Sending out mailers for invitation to services and church events
- Conducting a block party as an outreach activity
- Conducting a new member class for new church members
- Conducting leadership training for church members
- Receiving church planting training in terms of a boot camp or basic training by the church planter
- Working full-time over part-time as the church planter
- Being assessed prior to the beginning of the church plant as the church planter
- Delegating leadership roles to church members

Again, many of these factors are touched upon in other chapters of this book. Or, if you find one that is not mentioned in this book, it will certainly be found in some of the resources in the bibliography.

OK, thanks for allowing us to "geek out" for a few moments and include a long list of bullet points based on statistical research that would bore most people to tears. But there's a reason why all of this matters. In a cultural sense, growth can be plausibly predicted based on certain factors. Certainly the kingdom of God is much more than factors and correlations. But it is senseless for us to have access to good information about what strong churches who are seeking to replicable are doing only to ignore it out of a wayward sense of piety.

The survivability of many churches comes down to this: living out spiritual truths in the tangible world. If we discover that churches with a midweek children's program normally see more conversion growth, then just take it for what it is—a statistical observation. But what you should not do is ignore it because you don't like midweek children's programs. These observations are here for us to see what aids growth, but perhaps it is also to help test your willingness to do what it takes to lead a church plant beyond your personal preferences so that a larger work can be done in God's kingdom. Church leaders who watch how God is moving in other places are often the ones watching God move in their own place.

> *The survivability of many churches comes down to this: living out spiritual truths in the tangible world.*

From Surviving to Thriving

This chapter has offered a lot of numbers—statistics, correlations, and lists. That's why we started with a story of actual planters with dreams about church multiplication—and about their noteworthy progress in that direction. Church planting is first and foremost about people, especially those who do not have an active relationship with God through Jesus Christ.

Earlier in this chapter we quoted Jon Ferguson expressing a desire to keep things simple. As we read the Book of Acts, this seems to be the pattern of the early church. Acts makes an easily overlooked point about Paul's interaction with his apprentice Timothy: "Paul wanted Timothy to go with him" (Acts 16:3). Jon Ferguson speculates about what it might have looked like for Paul to reproduce himself through an apprentice like Timothy.

- I do. You watch. We talk.
- I do. You help. We talk.
- You do. I help. We talk.
- You do. I watch. We talk.
- You do. Someone else watches.
- The cycle now repeats for both Paul and Timothy.

We wonder if it's as simple and hard as that. But after all, it is the pattern established from 2 Timothy 2:2 where Paul writes to Timothy, "And what you have heard from me in the presence of many witnesses, commit to faithful men who will be able to teach others also." As it has already been stated by others, a good measure of success is when your church has grandchildren.

What if everyone in every church was involved in a disciple-making relationship? What if the people ahead of us were always showing us what they've learned, empowering us to do it, and encouraging us to pass it on to someone else? Would that be enough, as the Holy Spirit blessed it, for churches to multiply, for lost people to be found, and for life-changing disciples to be made?

Having a good survival rate is fine for those keeping a small scorecard. It sounds like a measure used by a scientist testing growth hormones on amoebas. But we are after more than just survival. We want your church to thrive to the point of mass multiplication. If you are finding triggers for growth within the lives of believers of your church, then expand the vision to become a group of believers

We want your church to thrive to the point of mass multiplication.

who birth new churches. Be willing to take it to the next level. Infuse a passion for planting other churches into the personal growth of believers in your church. When we raise the standard, then we unleash the providential potential inherent in believers for God to make them into a church planting movement.

8

HOUSE CHURCHES

Separating Reality from Fiction

Leadership Network Numbers

- **How Church Participation Is on the Rise**

The number of Americans involved in house churches is growing, according to comparative surveys conducted between 2005 and 2009. The increase is for both occasional and regular house church attenders.[1]

- **Approximately Two Million Go to a House-Type Congregation Rather Than a Conventional Church**

In a survey of 3,600 American adults, 1.4 percent attend a group of twenty or less "to pray and study scriptures" but also "rarely' or "never" attend a place of worship. Extrapolating that finding to the approximately 55 percent of America's 310 million residents identifying themselves as Protestant, then this translates to roughly 2 million people. The study may represent the purest measure of those who are not involved in an organized church, synagogue, or mosque but still are involved in some alternative faith community like, in the Christian faith, a house church.[2]

We need better assessment. We need more seminary-trained church planters. We need better coaching systems. Previous chapters talked about all these issues.

We envision a day when we do church planting with all the excellence and effort that makes church planting work better. It will involved funded teams, seminary training, denominational support, network involvement, and more.

But that won't be enough. While it could get us to church multiplication, it won't get us to a true movement. As we said in Chapter One, a church multiplication movement is *a rapid reproduction of churches planting churches measured by a reproduction rate of fifty percent through the third generation of churches, with new churches having fifty percent new converts. To achieve such momentum, churches would need to plant, on average, a new church every two years with each church reaching at least half of its attendees from the unchurched community.*

In Chapter Four, we compared that with David Garrison's definition of a church planting movement: a rapid and multiplicative increase of indigenous churches planting churches within a given people group or population segment.

If we experience a church multiplication movement, it will involve a huge surge in church planting as we have described it throughout the book. It will also require us to open up some new ways to plant churches.

We believe this will require a two-track approach. We need more church plants like we have seen them here—just done more and done better. But we need more church planting like what we have seen in church planting movements around the world. That's two tracks.

Our present system for starting new churches is like the checkout line at Walmart. But the store has only one lane open, and it's terribly backed up. Furthermore, this open lane is one that requires full-time church planters with up-front money.

This book is about the idea of opening up new lanes. Those lanes need to be different, such as one that gives permission to laypeople to start churches. Another lane could be for bivocational church planters. There are many more lane possibilities, but the first step is for more attention to changing the idea that one lane is sufficient! As our friend Scott Thomas of Acts 29 reminded us, "When we see the Great Commission as merely planting a single church we miss the vision for multiplication."

Global church planting movements are generally unencumbered by buildings, paid clergy, and denominational credentialing processes. We have not seen such movements here (since 1810). We believe that this new track is needed. As of now, such organic approaches have not produced the breakthrough needed. Regrettably, we have seen some claim to be church planting movements in the West, but the claims have failed to live up to scrutiny. But there are some glimmers of hope.

We believe they can work. It will "open up some more lanes" and "lay a second track"—and that is what it will take to get to a church multiplication movement and, we pray, perhaps even a true church planting movement one day. One of the faces of this new track will perhaps be organic or house church networks that have a strong DNA of multiplication.

House-Type Churches Started Early

For the first three centuries of Christianity, followers of Jesus commonly met in homes. U.S. Christians today who intentionally meet together in homes or locations other than a church building usually do so because of a desire to follow what they see as the original model founded by the apostles in the New Testament. They believe that small extended family–size churches were the pattern intended by Jesus Christ and modeled by the early church.

After Jesus' death, the Apostles gathered not in the temple but in an upper room. The New Testament repeatedly provides examples of house churches such as 1 Corinthians 16:19, "Aquila and Priscilla greet you heartily in the Lord, along with the church that meets in their home." Such statements lead some to conclude that the New Testament church was primarily a house church movement.

Today those associated with house churches are characterized or satirized as something very different. Often they are pictured as the strange people in clandestine meetings, making their own clothes, storing food in the basement, and preparing for the inevitable breakdown of society. House churches have typically been associated with those outside the mainstream of religious life in America.

But that is not really the case—most of the time. In reality, the term *house church* or *home church* is a generic reference to a small informal assembly of Christians, usually Protestant evangelicals, who intentionally gather in a home or similar convenient location other than a church building. Participants in house churches typically worship, pray, learn, and care for one another on an intensely personal level. House churches place emphasis on participation by everyone in the group and on sharing life together with a sense of community and mission that extends beyond meeting times. House churches are not the same as small groups or cell groups that are associated with a conventional church. House churches may network with other house churches, but each views itself as a complete church, not a subunit of a larger church. If small groups are a facet, then a house church is the entire stone. Some see themselves as a deliberate alternative to a traditional or established church.

House churches go by many different terms, some chosen to avoid the word "house" or "home" in order to put less emphasis on their location and more weight on the type of meeting that takes place. Common alternate titles used to describe this movement are simple church, open church, organic church, relational church, primitive church, body life church, micro church, *koinos* church (from the Greek word meaning all things in common) and biblical church.[3]

Neil Cole's Emphasis on Multiplication

Whatever name it goes by, the house church movement is growing in influence in the United States. One of the more influential
and effective house church networks is Church Multiplication
Associates led by Neil Cole, author of several books including
Organic Church, Organic Leadership, and *Church 3.0*.[4] As you can
tell, Church Multiplication Associates prefers a particular word
even to the point that they prefer the term "organic church" to
describe their expression. One of Cole's sayings is that "simple"
empowers Christians.
He's passionate that the
church can and should
be simpler, more organic
and easy to reproduce.
"We must lower the bar
of how we do church and
raise the bar on what it

> *"We must lower the bar of how we do church and raise the bar on what it means to be a disciple."*
>
> —NEIL COLE

means to be a disciple," he often says. He says that normal, ordinary people should take the lead in planting new churches.

Cole doesn't have many specific numbers to talk about. "If
you are successful in a multiplication movement, than you cannot
count them … if you can count them, you are not a multiplication
movement," he says.[5] But his movement, launched in 2002 with
the planting of ten churches, followed by eighteen in the second
year, fifty-two in the third, and over a hundred in the fourth, has
multiplied to thousands of churches today.

Church Multiplication Associates does regular training
throughout the year, figuring that their total pool of graduates
is planting between one to two churches a day, and the numbers
rise significantly when you consider daughter, granddaughter and
great-granddaughter churches. Their planters are now in over forty
states in the United States and over forty nations in the world.
What an amazing fact! Especially if you—like many leaders—have

a personality which is given to highly structured organizations and a belief that even Spirit-led movements need a little bit of planning.

Yet the leadership of Church Multiplication Associates has chosen decentralization, which, they say, is more "organic." No concentrated effort is made to watchdog or micromanage. Cole told us, "We just scatter the seed and water it and let it grow without any claim of authority over them."

Cole does not want his church planters' goal to be a big church; he urges them to develop a reproducing one. He is concerned about reaching people and making disciples, not with the number and longevity of his churches. "If a church lasts one year and gives birth twice, it is a success," he says.[6]

Ed and Warren, along with lead writer Elmer Towns, coauthored *Eleven Innovations in the Local Church*, which included a chapter on the house church movement in the United States. In our section on Neil Cole, we observe that he boils down the principles of the organic church to three simple ideas:

1. What we are doing isn't working.
2. What's really happening around the world tends to be in house churches.
3. If multiplication is our desire, it needs to be simple, transferable and ordinary.

For Cole, that simplicity boils down to the right DNA:

D—Divine Truth
N—Nurturing Relationships
A—Apostolic Mission[7]

"The apostolic heart in our group," Cole says, "originating in changed lives, regularly reminds us that God works as ordinary people are called to do the extraordinary. We don't *go* to church; we *are* the church."[8]

With such statements as this, Cole represents a positive uptick in the ecclesiology of today's planting environment. The house church movement was once seen as the "island of misfit toys," but now it is recapturing its theological foundation to once again represent the "city of God." Such an emphasis on the true meaning of *church* will be helpful for every leader hoping to spur a church multiplication movement.

> *The house church movement was once seen as the "island of misfit toys," but now it is recapturing its theological foundation to once again represent the "city of God."*

Lots of Participants, Lots of Variety

Until recently most Christians in America would have said that the count of house churches in the United States is very low. Frequently holding to an anti-organizational nature, the number of people in house churches makes it somewhat challenging to find them and almost impossible to count them. An Internet Google search lists at least two hundred house church organizations (individual house churches tied loosely together). Mike Steele, former director of DAWN (Disciple a Whole Nation) in the United States, identified almost 150 *networks* of house churches, each comprising many individual churches. For example, the Xenos Fellowship of Columbus, Ohio, has more than 110 house churches in that regional area.

In 2006 George Barna released a book titled *Revolution* that named house churching as a "seminal transition that may be akin to a third spiritual awakening in the U.S."[9] And that was one of his tamer statements. You can imagine that the book caused quite a stir among the church leadership community. In the book he numbers in the millions the people who participate in house churches, including those who also participate in traditional churches.

Secular media responded by doing articles and segments on the idea of the house church, heightening its level of exposure and acceptance.

Not everyone agrees with Barna's numbers or conclusions, but even a cautious survey puts the number of active participants at about two million (see Leadership Network Numbers mentioned earlier). The bottom line is that for a rapidly growing number of Americans, a local church is no longer the place to go as their primary religious meeting place. Nontraditional forms of religious experience and expression are growing in popularity and drawing millions of people closer to God but farther away from involvement in a typically structured church. More Americans are embracing various alternatives to a conventional church experience as being fully biblical, and at least according to some surveys, house churches are more satisfying to attenders than are conventional churches.

But Can They Multiply? Do They?

According to a 2006 survey by the Barna Group, 80 percent of house churches meet every week. The most common meeting days are Wednesday (27 percent) and Sunday (20 percent). Most house churches are family oriented; the average size of a house church is twenty people, including seven children under the age of eighteen. The typical house church gathering lasts for about two hours, with practices including:

- 93 percent have spoken prayer during their meetings.
- 90 percent read from the Bible.
- 89 percent devote time to sharing personal needs or experiences.
- 85 percent spend time eating and talking before or after the meeting.
- 83 percent discuss the teaching provided.

- 76 percent have a formal teaching time.
- 70 percent incorporate music or singing.

The rapid growth in house-church activity is evident in the fact that 54 percent of the people who are currently engaged in an independent home fellowship have been participating for less than three months. In total, 75 percent of house church participants have been active

> *75 percent of house church participants have been active in their current gathering for one year or less.*

in their current gathering for one year or less. One out of every five adults involved has been in their house church for three years or more.

House churches find new people. It's as simple as that. Now, retention is another story for another book. But let's be clear, if you want your church—house, traditional, organic, or conventional—to grow into a movement, then you will always need one crucial element: PEOPLE!

The house church model certainly produces a simple paradigm that is easily replicated, capable of having a strong evangelistic and disciple-making influence on people without a cumbersome structure. But has it developed the escape velocity needed to deliver on that ideal? In other words, will this iteration of house churches grow, catch attention, but ultimately fall back to earth like the iteration before them? Or this time will it have staying power? More directly, house churches, by their nature, are able to multiply, but do they actually do so?

To date, as we chronicle in more detail in our chapter in *Eleven Innovations in the Local Church*, the North American house church movement has largely been a reform movement, drawing mostly from existing believers who want something "better" than and "different" from what they currently have. Of course, "better" and "different" are highly relative terms. With only a few exceptions house church participants have been more excited about the "house" (the fellowship part) than the "church" (making and congregationalizing new disciples). They tend to gather more because of a desire to go deeper on some issue, whether it's Calvinism, charismatic practice, participative worship, or something else, but rarely is that issue a passion for evangelistic reproduction. Too many house churches lack a heart or track record for outreach beyond the existing fold of disenchanted Christians.

> *House church participants have been more excited about the "house" (the fellowship part) than the "church" (making and congregationalizing new disciples).*

Furthermore, to our knowledge, no house church movement, even when it's gained traction, has survived the death of its leader without changing its form or making substantive adjustments. Even for self-described revolutionaries within the modern church, a leader is desired. For house churches to find their formula for multiplication, their equation needs one more element. They need what all movements need: leadership multipliers with the intent of loss. When leaders are raised up who are willing to sacrifice size, resources, and other leaders for the sake of staring new gatherings, we will then witness a multiplication movement. The tipping point arrives when the emphasis is on the church and not the house.

By the way, we have written before (in *Eleven Innovations*) that we believe there are marks of a Biblical church. Although this is not an ecclesiology textbook (that is Ed's project in 2011), the way we do church matters. Churches need to be, well, biblical churches. That absolutely does not require buildings, budgets, and programs, but it does require things like biblical leadership, covenant community, practicing the ordinances, and several others. But if a church has those marks, it is a church regardless of whether it meets in a condo, a coffee shop, or a cathedral.

Some Bright Spots

Although house churches have learned to rapidly multiply in other parts of the world, they haven't done so to date in countries like the United States that are part of western industrialized democracies (more about that in Chapter Twelve). However, we see some groups trying to focus on replication through house church planting. One of those at the head of the pack is Neil Cole's Church Multiplication Associates, with their particular approach to an organic church model.

As part of the Leadership Network research project, Ed did a survey of ninety-seven of Church Multiplication Associates' planters, finding that fifty-three of fifty-four churches had planted a church in the previous year. This is *Fifty-three of fifty-four churches had planted a church in the previous year.* a most promising figure. The statistic shows a willingness for leaders to move or help others move to new spiritual gatherings. If this trajectory continues, it indeed could help birth a genuine church multiplication movement in America.

The other findings from the survey were equally promising. Of those who say their churches have helped start new churches in the last five years:

- 30 percent have started six or more new churches
- 22 percent have started at least one new church
- 11 percent have started two churches
- 18 percent have started three churches

- 9 percent have started four churches
- 9 percent have started five churches

Training Is Definitely Taking Place

When asked whether they are being coached or trained:

- 82 percent have been mentored or coached by another individual
- 79 percent say that they have received discipleship training in a local (institutional) church.
- 70 percent of organic church leaders say they have had at least some formal Bible college or seminary training.

To see such a high level of mentoring taking place makes sense in house churches. After all, it is their intention to live out their faith in close relational proximity to one another.

Discipleship Is Central

You can tell a lot about a movement by what it discusses—and how often. When asked how often they communicate regarding important values of the church, organic church leaders say they address the following key values to the church on a weekly or monthly basis:

- 97 percent—relationship with Christ
- 97 percent—importance of prayer
- 86 percent—maturing as a disciple
- 85 percent—reading the Bible
- 60 percent—personal evangelism
- 35 percent—mission service (35 percent mention it monthly)

- 26 percent—starting new churches (40 percent address it monthly)
- 18 percent—group evangelism (29 percent address it monthly)

One challenge in the model that the survey hinted at is the way the D (divine truth), N (nurturing relationships) and A (apostolic mission) are balanced. Cole would say they're feeding into a church planting movement, seeing some proto-movement activity, but he has affirmed there is a need for more intentional evangelism and multiplication.

We believe that if 40 percent of organic church leaders do not address personal evangelism during a typical month, then there is work that needs to be done. Neil Cole often says that churches still need a bigger kick in the "A" of their DNA (and by that, of course, he means "apostolic"). We agree—in all kinds of churches, including organic ones.

In general, the simple, replicable, permission-giving, lostness-sensitive approach of house churches could lead, we are convinced, to a wide-scale church multiplication movement. However, for that to happen, house church leaders need to be as passionate about the "church" as they are about the "house." In other words, their passion for lostness needs to exceed their passion for a new way of doing church. And, we think it is not there yet—even though if anyone is leading the way, Neil Cole is.

> *The simple, replicable, permission-giving, lostness-sensitive approach of house churches could lead, we are convinced, to a wide-scale church multiplication movement.*

9

MULTISITE STRATEGY

A Fast-Growing Trend That Affects Planting

Leadership Network Numbers

- **Many New Churches Are Using a Multisite Model**

    Among new churches surveyed, 11 percent are multisite. Many multisite churches are using, or planning to use, the additional sites as a means to church planting. Churches already doing multisite indicated that their primary intent was to reach otherwise unreachable areas from their primary location.[1]

- **Multisite and Church Planting Overlap Significantly in Large Churches**

    According to a national study of megachurches, 84 percent of those with satellite campuses have planted one or more other churches, compared to 74 percent that do not have satellite campuses.[2]

In 1997, Eric Disher founded Lexington (North Carolina) Community Church in a meeting room at the local YMCA. In 2009 the growing nondenominational, contemporary Christian church opened a second location in an old textile mill. Volunteers in the congregation, with average worship attendance of eight hundred at the time, had transformed the mill into a modern sanctuary.

Disher describes his church, now with its "north campus," as a multisite church. "It's really one church with two locations," he explains. "Our goal . . . is to multisite again and again." He already has a time line in mind. "We expect to add more locations within a year or two, or at least that's our hope," he says.[3]

Lexington Community Church is not alone in wanting to add location after location in order to reach more people. Across the continent, churches are going multisite, the vast majority doing so for evangelistic reasons. Planters are drawn to the concept as well. Many are actually front-loading this idea into their initial planning for the first plant. They want to take their church closer to the people they want to reach. Sometimes they want to stylize the church, through the additional site or sites, to speak the Gospel in a way that's tailored to a local neighborhood or a particular type of people.

Warren has headed several major research projects on multisite churches and coauthored two books, *The Multi-Site Church Revolution* and *The Multi-Site Church Roadtrip*.[4] LifeWay Research, which Ed directs, has likewise been involved in multisite research, producing *Multi-Site Churches* by LifeWay researcher Scott McConnell (including a foreword by Ed Stetzer).[5] The clear trend is that an increasing number of church planters are using multisite to launch their new churches. Though not technically church planting, it follows many characteristics of church planting.

An increasing number of church planters are using multisite to launch their new churches.

What about the theological implications of multisite? As Warren affirms in *The Multi-Site Church Roadtrip*, for hundreds if not thousands of churches, the biblical pulse behind multisite is as noncontroversial as reading the Great Commission (Matthew 28:19–20) and Great Commandment (Matthew 22:37–40), and deciding that multisite offers increased ways to share the Gospel. They also view new campuses as creating the environments described in Jesus' parables where lost sheep and coins are sought out, and where lost children are welcomed home (Luke 15). They want to take big risks for God that don't violate Scripture, identifying with apostle Paul's dream that "by all possible means I might save some. I do all this for the sake of the gospel" (1 Corinthians 9:22–23, NIV).

Are there potential liabilities to the idea of multisite? Certainly. Some critics have theological concerns about separating the traditional pastor-teacher role into two people. The typical way this happens in multisites is for one person or team—embodied by the lead pastor—to take responsibility for the church's teaching ministry. Meanwhile another person or team—embodied by the campus pastor—focuses on the local shepherding and ministry deployment needed at each local campus. This division of roles is an important issue for a congregation and its leadership to process.

We've seen that several churches that were once involved in church planting have now moved exclusively to multisite. That is a concern for us.

Others raise questions as to whether a multisite campus can contextualize adequately to its local community (and there are good and bad examples to ponder). If the new campus uses the preaching themes, children's ministry curriculum, and other resources of the sending campus, then will it be restricted in adapting to the distinctive qualities of the campus's neighborhood?

Others raise questions about leadership development: do multisites do a better or worse job of training and empowering the congregation for ministry engagement? Some of those concerned about the long-term implications of multisite suggest that it may limit reproduction of leadership, lead to a loss of evangelism, and produce spectators rather than disciples and leaders. Our observations show that there are some cases where this is true—and others where it is not. Either way, these are serious concerns to monitor, and discerning observers look before they leap. But, for us, we want to share some of the examples that do well—knowing and addressing the concerns we mention—and that see multiplication as part of their DNA.

Church Planting Versus Campus Launching

Seacoast Church in Charleston, South Carolina, went multisite in 2002 and today has thirteen campuses across South Carolina, North Carolina, and Georgia, and a weekend worship attendance of ten thousand. Seacoast's pastor, Greg Surratt, also has a vision for planting new churches. The same year Seacoast launched its first off-site campus, it cofounded the Association of Related Churches (ARC), a church planting organization that has planted almost a hundred congregations to date.[6]

Satellites *and* Church Planting Networks

Many churches are following a similar methodology as Seacoast in developing a growing multisite base and also a parallel church planting network. Among those introduced thus far in this book are Redeemer Presbyterian Church (Chapter Five), Mars Hill Church (Chapter Six), Hill Country Bible Church (Chapter Six), and Community Christian Church (Chapter Seven). These and many more are listed in the Appendix.

Some church leaders ask about the difference between creating a new campus and planting a totally separate new church. The idea of one church in multiple locations means that you share a common vision, budget, leadership, and board. If your new campus has a vision, budget, leader, or board that's not part of the sending campus, then in our view you've planted a new church or mission campus, not a multisite campus.

If your new campus has a vision, budget, leader, or board that's not part of the sending campus, then in our view you've planted a new church or mission campus, not a multisite campus.

In our early days of church planting, we would have relished the opportunity for someone else to carry the responsibilities of budgeting, administration, and the like for us. Multisite is not just about finding the next coolest place to pull off the next coolest music style in worship. It is a variation on collaboration that is leading some churches more quickly to the destination of multiplication.

Why do some churches choose to become multisite rather than spin off new churches? Here are some of the advantages of being part of a multisite:

- Accountability
- Sharing of resources (stewardship)
- Infusion of trained workers
- Shared DNA (vision and core values)
- Greater prayer support
- Preestablished network for problem solving
- No need to "reinvent the wheel"
- Connection with others doing the same thing

Satellites *as* Church Planting Networks

Could multisite also be an effective church-planting model? Absolutely. Many are doing just that, such as New Hope Christian

Fellowship, a Foursquare-related church pastored by Wayne Cordeiro in Honolulu, Hawaii. In 2000, New Hope began its first off-site video venue in order to open up room at the twelve-hundred-seat high school auditorium that the church rents weekly for worship services. Some people were initially reluctant to try the off-site service, but Cordeiro says within a year, "It became so popular that we moved to two Sunday services there. Within the next three years, we began video venues in seven off-site locations."

For Cordeiro, the satellite breakouts are part of an intentional church planting plan. "Our goal for satellites is not necessarily to add locations. It is to develop new leaders. It is to ease these emerging leaders into their own teaching where one day we can release them as standalone churches," he says. Once again, development of leadership is an inescapable factor for church multiplication movements. "When young leaders go out with this model, they have time to build relationships, develop teams, think about evangelism projects, do community outreach, and build leaders."

> *Development of leadership is an inescapable factor for church multiplication movements.*

Many of Cordeiro's local campuses serve as campuses of New Hope Community Church. Some are blessed to become self-standing churches, usually still part of the Foursquare denomination and describing themselves as "affiliates" of New Hope.

For efforts beyond Honolulu, the church plants often affiliate with a network formerly called New Hope International and now coordinated through the School of Church Planters, which is part of New Hope's Pacific Rim Bible College. No matter the affiliation, Cordeiro and New Hope church are always on ready-set-go for another church site to be established.

Deciding Whether to Plant a Church or Launch a Campus

This is a book about church planting, not multisite. But in some places they intentionally and strategically overlap. We acknowledge that sometimes multisite is an opportunity for a rock star senior pastor to project his image in front of additional passive followers. But we also see many churches being passionate about multisite *and* church planting. So we thought it helpful to affirm them and talk about how they do so.

How does a church decide whether to follow the "and" or the "as" option? There are no set rules. For Seacoast, the decision came down to two basic questions:

1. What Are the Gifts and Passion of the Leader?

The leader's gifts and passion are always the starting place for determining whether to plant a church or launch a campus.

Seacoast has two stories about determining leadership in an individual. First, when Naeem Fazal, one of Seacoast's young adult leaders, began talking about a desire to start new work in Charlotte, North Carolina, we knew that he was an ideal church planter. Fazal was an outstanding speaker with a unique vision to build a multi-ethnic ministry, so the church connected him with the Association of Related Churches and helped him launch Mosaic Church, www.mosaicchurch.tv.

Second, however, when Seacoast leaders talked with Ron Hamilton, they saw a different gifting and passion. Hamilton was a founding member of the church and had helped form the DNA as a member of the leadership team. Although comfortable communicating from the stage, Hamilton's real gifts lay in building leaders and empowering teams. Hamilton was an ideal campus pastor, and he now leads Seacoast's campus in West Ashley, South Carolina.

2. What Is the Proximity of the New Congregation to an Existing Campus or Church Plant?

Seacoast tries not to plant new churches in close proximity to existing Seacoast campuses because they believe it can create confusion among members when they are asked to choose between their church and the new plant. With a new campus, however, the people who attend from the sending campus do not have to make a choice. They are not leaving their current church; just as someone in a large traditional church might choose between "early" and "late" churches on Sunday morning, they are simply attending a different service. To avoid confusion, Seacoast asks church planters to choose a community at least a hundred miles from an existing church plant or campus.

Big Vision, Denominations Welcome

Multisite is not limited to individual churches as they start a new site which then becomes a separate church in its own right. Often the bigger the vision, the more likely the church is to experiment with multisite or church planting as a way to fulfill it.

Hill Country Bible Church, a nondenominational congregation introduced for its internship program in Chapter Six, is a church with both multiple campuses and also the Hill Country Association, a church planting network. The Texas-based congregation has a vision that every person in the Austin area will hear the good news of Jesus from a member of a Hill Country church. "Since there are over 1.4 million people in the Austin area that means we will have to plant a lot more churches a lot faster!" senior pastor Tim Hawks told us. Churches like that, over time, often function like quasi-denominations.

But denominations are endorsing this approach as well. Both the Assemblies of God and Evangelical Free Church have included multisite in their church planting training and strategy. As a few denominations are willing to encourage such innovative thinking, then others will begin to follow suit. We should all be encouraged whenever we see denominational leaders searching for new ways to expand God's kingdom as it is expressed in their own tribe of churches.

Not Either-Or but Both-And

The explosion over the last five years of both new church plants and new multisite churches has been phenomenal, and the lines between the two are becoming more and more blurred. In the end, church planting doesn't have to be an either-or question. Instead, as Seacoast, Community Christian, New Hope, West Ridge and others have demonstrated, it can be a both-and.

As Bob Hyatt, pastor of Evergreen Community in Portland, Oregon, said in a 2009 interview, multisite often leads to church planting. Multisite "is a step towards church planting," he says. "It gives us all the benefits of a church plant without most of the risk. It's something new in a new space, yet doesn't have to be instantly self-sustaining."[7]

Likewise, Larry Osborne, who has pioneered a video-venue approach to multisite at North Coast Church in Vista, California, says, "It's a both-and world. We need church plants and multisite. . . . If I have a gifted communicator, I tell them to plant. If I have someone who is a good shepherd, I suggest multisite."[8]

Furthermore, some denominations, such as the Assemblies of God, believe that church multiplication takes place through both sites *and* plants—and in 2009 they created a new category named "parent-affiliated" congregations as a way of reporting these congregations.

The bottom line is: We believe that God is calling your church to be a part of the multiplication movement. How are you going to do it?

10

RAPID GROWTH

Still Not Reproduction

Leadership Network Numbers

- **Fast-Growing Churches Start Larger**

    75 percent of fast-growing churches had over a hundred people in attendance at the first service; for churches that did not grow as fast, less than 20 percent had over a hundred at their first service.[1]

- **Fast-Growing Churches Tend to Be Contemporary in Worship Style**

    75 percent of fast-growing church plants used a contemporary style of worship. Churches that did not grow as fast are more equally distributed through the categories of traditional, contemporary, and blended styles.[2]

- **Fast-Growing Churches Invest Outwardly**

    80 percent of fast-growing churches put 10 percent of their budgets toward outreach and evangelism; only 42.3 percent of churches that grew at slower rates committed this amount. Also 63 percent of fast-growth churches raised additional funding; this compares dramatically to 23 percent in those that didn't grow as fast.[3]

In many people's minds, a rapidly growing church is the same as multiplication. Sometimes it is, but not always. Consider this scenario: within the first four months of your church's birth, over forty people trust Jesus Christ to be their personal Savior. After the first year, the church's growth moved it to two services. Within two years, the growth necessitated the move into a bigger facility. What if by the church's tenth year, new professions of faith had not let up and weekly attendance was over three thousand? It happened to one pastor and his answer was to build change into the system as the only normal option.

"From day one we have told people never to get comfortable because you never know when things are going to change," says Brian Bloye, lead pastor of West Ridge Church, based thirty miles northwest of Atlanta in the growing suburb of Dallas, Georgia. We briefly introduced this church in the discussion in Chapter Six of training materials for church planters. But now we want to underscore its growth trajectory, as "God continues to amaze us," according to Bloye.

West Ridge is itself a church plant, born in 1997 as a daughter church of First Baptist Church of Woodstock, Georgia. Although the church is having a significant impact in Atlanta's northwest suburbs, its bigger impact may be the new churches that have launched from their ministry. It wants to do for others what First Baptist of Woodstock did for it. As a result, West Ridge has been instrumental in planting almost fifty churches throughout the country, including several in the Atlanta region.

West Ridge has been instrumental in planting almost fifty churches throughout the country including several in the Atlanta region.

Big Is Bad If It's Anti-Small

We suspect some readers turned first to this chapter of *Viral Churches*, anticipating that it will contain the real heart-of-the-book message. You were perhaps aware that we've both done quite a bit of study about megachurches. Ed, working through LifeWay Research, has researched and written *Outreach* magazine's "Top 100" lists in recent years. Warren's megachurch research through Leadership Network (see www.leadnet.org/megachurch) has gotten him quoted in major newspapers across the country.

So maybe you're expecting us to beat up on larger churches like you would a low-hanging piñata on Cinco de Mayo. You're thinking we should fuss at those megachurches who grow by attracting good people from smaller churches and extol those who stay focused on spiritual outreach into their communities and social efforts to make their communities a better place.

If so, you're wrong. We rejoice when disciples of Jesus Christ are made and matured in churches of all sizes, including big churches. We gladly acknowledge that a good number of really big churches got that way because their hearts beat powerfully with a concern to reach people who have a broken relationship with God. We know that angels rejoice in heaven "over one sinner who repents" (Luke 15:10), not when the saints are merely reshuffled from one church to another. We also think it's absolutely the right direction when big churches become more missional, eager for this verse to describe their reputation in the community: "In the same way, let your good deeds shine out for all to see, so that everyone will praise your heavenly Father" (Matthew 5:16, NLT).

Our caution about big churches is that the more they grow, the more likely they are to grow by addition rather than multiplication. It is never easy to give up the people and resources necessary to multiply. The larger a church becomes the greater the temptation becomes to take on a sedentary position to movemental Christianity. The larger the church, the less able

In reality, a church grows bigger by doing small better.

it is to multiply itself—unless its leaders continually make heroes of small replicable groups, teams, or classes. In reality, a church grows bigger by doing small better.

Church multiplication movements are enlarging God's kingdom as the yeast Jesus describes in his parables. "The kingdom of heaven is like yeast that a woman took and mixed into 50 pounds of flour" (Matthew 13:33) "until it spread through the entire mixture" (Luke 13:21). In short, these churches rapidly multiply and transform what is around them. We should value the movements of the small that are overtaking large ground for the kingdom.

Ed was recently the interim teaching pastor for two years at a growing megachurch. He made this same point in one of his final sermons (and his time there did not end because of this sermon!). Using the mustard seed and yeast parables found back-to-back in Matthew 13:31–33, he made these points:

1. *The kingdom of God starts small,* showing up in the person of Jesus and in small groups where he is present (Matthew 18:20). Most people in his day were surprised that God's kingdom didn't show up big. Even John the Baptizer seemed confused because he was expecting something big (Matthew 11:2). So were the Pharisees who had to be reminded that "The kingdom of God is not coming with something observable; no one will say, 'Look here!' or 'There!' For, you see, the kingdom of God is among you" (Luke 17:20).

2. *The kingdom of God becomes big,* so big that it is shocking. It grows from Jesus being born in a manger to today when over a billion people around the world identify themselves as his followers. Multiplication movements are the same. They begin with an infancy which promises nothing but one day—BOOM!—the unexpected and incredible happens.

3. *The kingdom of God then permeates its environment,* transforming it in good ways. God is interested in redeeming all things. When God's kingdom moves, it changes not only individuals but the community and culture as well.

The point related to church multiplication? It's easier to come and watch a show than it is to go and serve. Jesus did not say the kingdom of heaven is like a group of people who sat and listened to people talk about him. He said it's like a mustard seed that was planted and grew. It's like yeast that permeates. Simple, small replicable units are how the kingdom is best advanced.

Simple, small replicable units are how the kingdom is best advanced.

In fact there are even social theories that explain how movements such as Christianity grow over these simple relational bridges. It starts with what scholars refer to as the "strength of *weak* ties"—your acquaintances can expand your relational world by introducing you to people you don't know, which links you to a variety of untapped social networks. As Harvard professor Stanley Milgram discovered, we are just six handshakes (or introductions) away from anyone on the planet. Then for a movement to grow, it must not only reach new people, but also retain them and grow them. That's where an underlying basis of *strong* relationships is present, such as a small group, service team, or Sunday school class. Movements that spread rapidly may appear to grow spontaneously and

Movements that spread rapidly usually proliferate within and across networks of relationships.

randomly, but on closer inspection they usually proliferate within and across networks of relationships.

We are reminded of Mark Twain's description of church: Good people sitting in front of good people telling them how to be good people. A church multiplication movement is more than a revival of morality. It is the advancement of God's kingdom against the gates of Hades. And we see small bands of believers working as some of God's lean, fighting forces rescuing those perishing in darkness.

But our era of history values "big" over "small" on a consistent basis. With new words like "ginormous" being popularized and used ad nauseam, we are a people who like big. But we must understand the danger inherent in attributing value to big without discernment. "Big" produces more consumers in church, but small produces more contributors. The most likely place for life transformation to take place is not in a big sanctuary, but in face-to-face small settings of accountability or service. There we can provoke one another

> *"Big" produces more consumers in church, but small produces more contributors.*

"to love and good works" (Hebrews 10:24). There we can ask, "How are you doing? How can you do better? How can we do it together?" There you can look a needy family in the eye as you compassionately feed them, clothe them, or help them to find a new job. Perhaps one reason the church is declining in North America is that we have forgotten that Jesus is working in the small.

Yeast permeates the bread mix, and in the process it changes the bread, transforming it into something else. Churches should permeate the community and change it. As we proclaim, serve, and show the good news of Jesus Christ, we will reshape our world in good ways. Paul uses a similar metaphor in 2 Corinthians 2:14, "But thanks be to God who always puts us on display in Christ and spreads through us in every place the scent of knowing Him." We're to spread the scent of knowing God, letting it permeate our families, neighborhoods, and workplaces.

We don't want to overstate the point, but we think Jesus is anti-big *when big replaces small.* Not because only one can be worthwhile to his kingdom but because *both* are worthwhile to his kingdom. Big is good and so is small, but only when they are reproducing beyond themselves. Based on our personal observations and the research, we think people best join Jesus in his kingdom mission when they get involved in the small. Small is often the place of the kingdom's agenda, the place to plant the mustard seed and to permeate the yeast.

What Good Things Accompany Rapid Growth?

Having put "big" in a context of "small," we're ready to look at churches that grow rapidly. Part of Ed's study for Leadership Network involved a partnership with researcher Stephen Gray to understand what factors led to churches passing two hundred people in attendance quickly—less than three years from launch.[4]

This fast growth in new churches is certainly not the norm. As we noted in the Leadership Network Numbers at the beginning of Chapter Seven, the average attendance of a church plant is seventy-three people after three years.

Steven Gray's study found twenty-one statistically significant factors where fast-growth churches differed with other new churches. (For his study, he compared sixty fast-growing church plants and fifty-two church plants that did not grow as fast.)

Training Made a Big Difference

In talking with Gray, the most important of his twenty discoveries dealt with leadership development. Gray's research bore out that whether a church grew fast or struggled, nearly 65 percent of planters received some type of training for their work. Fast-growing and struggling plants both received training—at about the same frequency. The real difference is in how much training they received. Fast-growing plants and planters were engaged in substantially more training—with statistical significance at every level.

> *Fast-growing plants and planters were engaged in substantially more training—with statistical significance at every level.*

Not only were planters trained and coached personally, but they did ministry in teams. An impressive 88 percent had church planting teams; in sharp contrast, only 12 percent of struggling church plants were planted by teams. They also built a core group before launch, with 63 percent having a core group of twenty-six to seventy-five people. By contrast among the other churches, nearly 70 percent had less than twenty-five in their core group.

In addition, planters had others encouraging and supporting them from the outside. Planters felt a greater sense of support from their pastoral colleagues and surrounding churches, had more fellowship with other pastors, their work was more highly celebrated by their denomination, and they experienced far less negativity from their direct superiors than those leading struggling church plants.

Though some pastored part-time, a slightly higher percentage (17 percent) of the church planters were full-time. The contrast comes out in the team factor: only 17 percent of fast-growing plants started with only one paid staff member, while over 90 percent of churches that did not grow as quickly had only one paid staff member at launch time.

Bigness Doesn't Guarantee Multiplication

This book proposes that the future of the church in America is not invested so much in big churches growing bigger and better, but in a massive multiplication movement of new church planting. Large churches, perhaps more than anyone else, can put muscle, money, and momentum into such an effort. Among many great characteristics of large churches, perhaps that is the best.

In other parts of this book, we have suggested that a change of the scorecard is needed to see a multiplication movement occur where you lead. We contend that if you change the scorecard in the church that eventually you will be able to change the scorecard in the community. Rather than seeking to be the next big thing—the church version of "America's Got Talent"—let's become the next transformative thing. Instead of our neighbors saying, "Wow, you've got a big church," let's create a movement where they say, "Wow—your church makes a difference all over our county." Or "all over our state." Or "across our entire nation."

A multiplication movement might not need help from big churches. But big churches do need to multiply their impact. Likewise, a multiplication movement does not need small churches. But small churches need to multiply their involvement. Bigness is never the point, unless you're speaking of the greatness of Christ and multiplying the number of people following him.

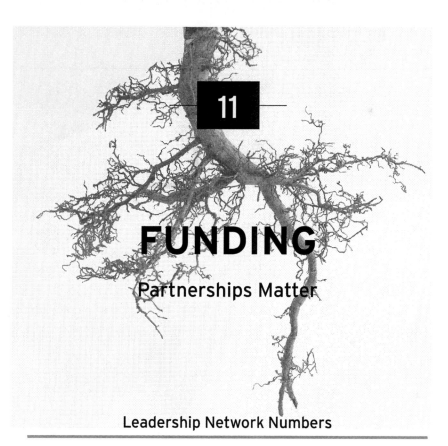

11

FUNDING

Partnerships Matter

Leadership Network Numbers

- **Some Churches "Tithe" to Church Planting**

  Many of the more aggressive parent churches assign 10 percent or more of their overall church budget to domestic church planting.

- **More Than One in Four Churches Have Financially Supported a New Church**

  According to a 2008 random poll of U.S. Protestant churches, 28 percent have directly participated in starting a new church in the last twelve months, in terms of providing direct financial support.[1]

- **Outside Funding Sometimes Discourages Church Parenting**

  More money from the national agency correlates with a *lower* percentage of churches that become parent churches.

- **Denominational Funding Is Partial and Lasts Thirty-two Months on Average**

  The average church planter who receives denominational funding for 32 months and is expected to raise one-third to one-half of support needed; 27 percent of planters are required to raise all support needed; 24 percent are fully funded through national, regional and local efforts; the fully funded percentage rises to 49 percent when the church planter's efforts are added to the national, regional, and local support.

E ver see a teenager driving a brand new sports car? Most of us see it and wonder, "Who paid for that car?" Or, in Ed's case, "What a waste!" No matter what your initial thought, it seems to beg the question of who is bankrolling a muscle car for someone who is just learning to drive.

With the launch of approximately four thousand new churches every year in the United States, the question on many minds is "Who's funding this?" Whereas simple churches are being started by the thousands with no upfront money in Third World countries, this is far less frequently the case in America. Most new ventures in the United States need and acquire various levels of financial support. Here is the breakdown of where that money originates.

Money from Denominational Sources

Without exterior funding, very little church planting would be accomplished outside of organic church models. In recent U.S. history the majority of the funds to launch new churches came from denominations. Today funding comes from a variety of sources but denominations continue to play an important role.

As Chapter Four explained, the emphasis on church planting is shifting from the initiative and oversight of a national or regional agency to that of the local church. The trend toward local church initiation includes funding and oversight of finances. With this shift to the local church, funding has also shifted from the national agency to the parent church and the church planter. National agencies are retooling to stand alongside regional and local church planting efforts to provide help in recruiting, assessment, training, and coaching in ways that involve lesser amounts of funding than in the past. After all, it is logical that if you find a competent candidate with a strong calling, funding will follow training.

Most denominational agencies have aggressive and measurable goals to increase the number of parent churches within their denominational circles. With this shift to the local church, funding has also shifted from the national agency to the parent church and the church planter.

The Lutheran Church Missouri Synod is a good illustration of the current trend. Funding typically includes national and judicatory (regional) portions. Until 2009, the judicatory funding could be up to $50,000 per year for three years and national funding peaked at a one-time grant of $50,000 to selected church plants. Whereas local entities are designated to keep track of church planting funds, circuits (a level under the district) also help to accomplish the funding.

For 2006–2008, the denomination's District New Partnerships/World Mission North America gave $605,000 toward "Ablaze! New Congregation Development Grants." Typically, support to a new congregation ranged from $15,000 to 25,000. Within their system, the calling entity provides the salary and benefits to new planters. The denomination will spend about $2,500 per week to train just one church planter. After formal training, a new church receives financial sponsorship for three years with the goal of the new church's becoming self-sufficient at the end of that period. However, most of the judicatories last three to five years. To maintain accountability for the funding they receive, planters submit regular reports to show that progress is being made in areas such as evangelism and ministry. The Lutheran Church Missouri Synod is actively funding churches but is aggressively seeking local congregations to support the local work of church planting.

Current trends in denominational funding for church planting feature the provision of Web-based distance learning for church planters featuring interaction with instructors, mentors, and peer coaching, plus the development of a validated Mission Initiation

Plan. This church planter training is also accessed by sponsoring congregations of the new church plants. In addition, the denomination has created a Revolving Mission Planting Fund which offers a low-interest loan of $150,000 spread over three to five years to churches sponsoring new church plants.

More Parent Churches

With the move toward recruiting parent churches to support church planting directly, in many cases the national and regional agencies provide no more than 33 percent (or often less) of funding needs. Thus the majority of funding tends to rest on the shoulders of the parent church and the church planter.

There also appears to be a correlation between the amount of money the national agency contributes to each church plant and the number of parent churches in that denomination. As noted in the "Leadership Network Numbers" section, more money from the national agency correlates with a *lower* percentage of churches that become parent churches. This is one of those "surprising but true" factoids of life. It reinforces to us that local churches must take up the work if we are to witness a multiplication movement on our continent.

Local churches must take up the work if we are to witness a multiplication movement on our continent.

Fully Funded or Partially Funded?

The financing of individual church plants is also in flux. On average, church planters receive financial support from their denomination for thirty-two months. The origination and level of financial support are important to note. Only 7 percent of planters are fully funded without any personal fund-raising required (funding could come through national, regional, and local efforts). Although 7 percent of survey respondents reported that their planters raise all of their own funding, the majority (55 percent) report that their planters receive denomination funds *and* raise their own support.

Typically, planters are expected to raise one-third to one-half of the support they need. A quarter (27 percent) are required to raise all of their financial support. Whether intentional or not, there is a consequent rise in the number of bivocational church planters.

As we have noted in other chapters, professional clergy are not necessary to have a biblical church. But they don't hurt either. Both organic and fast-growing conventional churches can be rapidly multiplying churches. It all depends on the perspective and vision of the leadership. Though money is a factor, it is not the only factor.

The average regional church planting budget is $246,346. (However, this figure is skewed because some regions report administrative budgets in their figures, while others leave that figure out.) The analysis provided to Leadership Network suggests that the average regional budget provided for direct support of all their church planters or all their church plants ranges from $75,000 to $125,000.

We are all grateful for the money that denominations are putting toward church planting, but we believe they need to do more—and do it more efficiently. Simply put, most denominations spend far more on maintenance than mission. They spend the vast majority of funds servicing existing churches rather than starting new ones.

> *Most denominations spend far more on maintenance than mission.*

Money from Church-Planting Networks

There is an obvious difference between the budgeting of a church planting network and that of a plant from a denominational agency. The budgets for church planting networks vary greatly. Only about 10 percent of the surveyed networks have an annual budget greater than $1,000,000. However, this range is much higher than the norm. The average annual budget for the remaining 90 percent of the networks is $182,500. In other words, denominations are like Fort Knox compared to the networks, which are more like a small-town bank.

The average amount of funding received by a new church plant for a network is $172,200. When they report their funding numbers, most networks mixed the total funds a church plant received (funding from the network plus planter's fundraising efforts), rather than reporting only the amount provided directly to the plant from the network. In other words, networks require the church planter to raise funds in addition to those provided by the network. For example, the Kairos Church Planting group in Portland, Oregon, reports that planters both receive funding and must raise individual funding from parent churches and personal relationship networks. Typically, this network will support a church plant financially for up to forty-eight months.

On the high end of funding, Sovereign Grace Ministries provides $110,000 to $120,000 for the average church plant. Of that, $60,000 comes from the Sovereign Grace mission fund with the rest from tithes and offerings of the founding families in the embryo church. Sovereign Grace Ministries normally sends out large groups of people to plant a church. In one instance, one hundred people relocated to a church plant in Denver. Sovereign Grace Ministries also offers one-year complete support and then evaluates whether help should be extended for a longer time period.

Priority on Coaching

Though many networks do not require coaching for their planters, most make it a priority. If you are giving away money, you want to know it is being used well. In some cases, the network funds the coaching or arranges for a network coach as part of the network relationship. Thus, some networks included their fee for personal coaching in their report of the planting process.

Organizations such as Griffith Coaching and New Church Initiatives provide coaching for planters during the prelaunch, launch, and immediate post-launch phases. Networks, denominations, and planters themselves will contract with these organizations for twelve to eighteen months at a cost of $2,000 to $6,000.

The Hill Country family of churches in Austin, Texas, have engaged New Church Initiatives which offers a coaching process for up to two years after launch. This process not only holds the planter accountable for staying focused, but provides guidance in the development and implementation of critical systems such as assimilation, spiritual formation, and leadership development. With their focus on the "missional" church, they also provide guidance for implementing local community development, global engagement, and church multiplication—which we really like.

While church planting networks provide a lot of support, they generally accept only 20 percent of those who apply to their church planting programs. The networks averaged twenty applicants a year but only five approvals.

Scott Thomas of the Acts 29 Network points out that they have about five hundred people in the application phase and "approximately 50 percent make it through the online preassessment interactions and phone interviews while around 50 percent of those are declined during the face-to-face interview. Our goal in the assessment is not to decline potential planters but rather to shepherd the applicants toward discerning God's will for them. Those not recommended to plant often thank us for our honest evaluation." In other words, approximately 25 percent go on to be Acts 29 church planters. Networks don't look to be stingy but they are looking to be discerning.

Money from Church Planting Churches

Churches that aggressively pursue church planting have a number of financial factors in common. Typically these churches expect

new church planters to raise a sizable amount of the church planting budget, commonly 50 to 80 percent. They also rely on their
respective denominations. However, as has been mentioned, the
majority of funding responsibility is trending toward the parent
church and church planter as the source, with the denomination
typically providing less than one-third of the needed funds.

Surprisingly, it appears that most of the aggressive, reproducing churches provide less financial support than do less aggressive
churches. Large investments into few places means fewer plants

*Large investments into few places
means fewer plants and a lessened
probability for a multiplication
movement.*

and a lowered probabil-
ity for a multiplication
movement. For exam-
ple, CrossPointe Church
in Orlando donates
12 percent of its budget
toward church planting.
On average, $25,000
is budgeted for each church plant. CrossPointe has participated
as a sponsor church in five plants directly and three others as a
part of a network. On the other hand, churches like Northwood
Church in Keller, Texas, put much less money into each individual
plant—but they plant six to eight and occasionally as many as ten
churches a year.

Many of the more aggressive parent churches assign 10 percent
or more of the overall church budget to domestic church planting.
Translated into dollars, the actual amount of money from some
of the larger churches is anywhere from $80,000 annually to over
$1,000,000.

Stewardship Training for the Core Group

One unique approach to funding can be found at Hill Country
Bible Church. The church encourages its planters to enlist ten
to twelve families from within their congregation to go as "missionaries" to help start each of their new churches. Part of the

commitment of this "missional core" is to support the new church financially with an initial "first fruits" donation, as well as with ongoing monthly support. Their planters are trained and required to disciple this missional core in financial stewardship prior to launch. In Chapter Twelve, you will see this element reflected as key to launching into a multiplying movement.

In addition to this "donation" of tithing families, Hill Country provides 100 percent of the planters' salary, benefits, and basic ministry expenses for a full year prior to launch. This funding period enables

The goal is for each planter to build a missional core of at least twenty lay missionaries who are "farming" the target community along with the church planter.

the planters to prepare personally through their residency program and to gather a following of unchurched people in their target communities. The goal is for each planter to build a missional core of at least twenty lay missionaries who are "farming" the target community along with the church planter. Between the planter and this missional core, Hill Country expects the cultivation of up to four hundred qualified prospects from the community for the new church.

By following this approach, the new church plant is well on its way to being self-sustaining. However, in addition to that, Hill Country still encourages its planters to find outside sources of funding and gives up to $50,000 support after launch. Hill Country plants multiple churches annually and hopes to plant even more per year in coming years.

A multistream approach to securing income for the church

A multistream approach to securing income for the church plant seems to be the most effective.

plant seems to be the

most effective. Tapping into finances from the denomination, mother church, and missional core gives the planting leader the most latitude to work with expandable resources.

Additional Funding Sources

You've heard the stories. Someone decides to plant a church in some large metropolitan area and before they know it, they have $250,000 for start-up money. Then we wonder, "Why didn't that happen to me?"

Where do church planters find financial support apart from their denomination, their mother church, or a church planting network? Some church planters are very resourceful, sometimes raising several hundred thousand dollars. However, for most planters, fund raising is a huge challenge. Apart from the sources cited here, the best channel for raising additional support is the planter's network of personal relationships. Many approach their home church or a church they served in some way. Others approach people whose lives they have touched through ministry. Many do all of the above.

Some planters network through their established relationships to form new relationships. A few approach private foundations. Hal Haller is a church planter in Florida who has been very effective at raising support and who trains other planters in fund-raising. "The sky is the limit," says Haller. "You must communicate to everyone that you are not only a pastor but a missionary."

If you want to gain enough money to start a church that starts a movement, then understand why people give. They give to great vision and trusted people. Resources always follow vision. Church planters must become very skilled at communicating vision. Also, people give to people; more than anything else, fund-raising is about relationships. Whether the source is the denomination, a network or organization, a mother church, a partner church, bivocational work, the early launch team, or other individuals, the key to soliciting support is through authentic relationships.

So what to do? The research suggests that it is best for an agency or denomination to fund a qualified and well-trained church planter with a modest funding package over a relatively short period of time (three years or less). It's "modest" so that the planter will seek to aggressively build the church. It's "over a short period time," so that the newly developing church will not become dependent on outside income. And it's given to someone with the calling to multiply.

Aggressive and highly effective church planters tend to be entrepreneurial and able to find creative means of funding the plant other than with direct assistance from denominational or church planting agencies.

Beyond salary assistance, church planters prefer assistance with church development and training resources—books, boot camp, assessment, conferences, and other helps.

Money Shortages Aren't the Real Problem

Ed's Ph.D. dissertation was an analysis of factors leading to more robust church plants. As part of the survey, he asked an open-ended question of what they would have done differently. The most common response is that they were part-time planters, but if they had been full-time their new church would have done better. The second most common response also involved money: if they would have had start-up funds, they would have been successful or more successful. Interestingly, those who did have start-up funds said that if they had even more to underwrite a staff team, they would have done better.

In short, everyone said that they could have done better. And all of them tied their lack of greater success to finances. Opinions of alternative futures can never be assumed as fact. But these responses tie into another factor that helps us determine whether a church planter will be around for many years to come: realistic expectations. When there is a lack of money, it is tempting to expect defeat.

Though we want to implicitly trust those working in the field, the actual research tells a different story. According to Ed's dissertation, factors related to higher attendance are assessment, mentoring, and training. It is interesting to note that the amount of funding had no correlation with successfully increasing attendance.

It is interesting to note that the amount of funding had no correlation with successfully increasing attendance.

In western industrialized nations, we typically associate security and successful launches with sufficient funds. Combining some of the lessons we've presented, we see that though money can be helpful, it is not paramount. Organic churches are multiplying all around the world with virtually no funding. Most multiplication movements happen without thought to funding because they are driven by the Holy Spirit who does not need our resources.

With this chapter, our intention is twofold. First, if you have money, then give it all away to church planting that is multiplication biased. Whether "you" are a denomination, church, or individual—make the decision that church multiplication is the great biblical evangelism strategy seen in Acts. Second, if you are a planter, then move forward no matter what. It is not trite or cliché to remember that God owns the cattle on a thousand hills. If God has called you, then God will indeed provide for you, though in his own time frame and in his way. The early church was a scattered, persecuted, and often poor band of believers. But by sharing their lives and by God's grace, they turned the Roman Empire upside down (or right-side up). Money is great, but it will be necessary for a movement only if God deems it to be so. And when God does, just ask him for it.

12

THE NEW SCORECARD

Measuring a Church Multiplication Movement

Leadership Network Numbers

- **Type of Model Isn't as Important as Emphasis on Multiplication**

The most effective church multiplication strategy clearly seems to be local churches (sometimes with help from denominations and networks) planting other churches—which in turn have church-planting DNA ingrained in them from their inception. "Churches . . . won't multiply churches until they have multiplied believers, leaders, and ministries. Then multiplication is natural and expected even at the church level." Phil Stevenson, Wesleyan Church Evangelism and Church Growth Department.[1]

NorthWood Church in Keller, Texas, has discovered that multiplication is better than addition, and exponential growth is more effective than self-expansion. Under the leadership of founding and senior pastor Bob Roberts, the twenty-five-year-old Texas church has planted over a hundred congregations in the past eighteen years. These churches are everywhere—nine are within a ten-mile radius of its own campus, while others are thousands of miles away. But most important, NorthWood, which is Southern Baptist, is producing churches that in turn produce more churches.

At the heart of its reproducing strategy is the NorthWood Church Multiplication Center, a nine-month intensive internship in which Roberts, who writes books with titles like *The Multiplying Church: The New Math for Starting New Churches* (see Bibliography), annually trains more than a dozen potential planters and their spouses. To ensure that they reach diverse communities worldwide, the church seeks to fill half its internships with non-Anglo planters who plan to multiply inside or outside North America. NorthWood also provides financial support to its internship graduates.

The new plants aren't limited to a specific model. Instead they include various church types—multisite, house church, and traditional. Rather than beginning with a specific model of church, the Church Multiplication Center trains its participants to focus on the needs of the community and adjusts its model accordingly.

The focus is on developing a faithful church that makes a difference in a local community but never finds a boundary marker where change stops. "We want to embed the ethos or DNA that we believe is essential for the planting of churches that will transform people and the world," Roberts explains. Key to achieving this goal is the teaching of global engagement through a required "other side of the world" trip that Roberts personally leads to such places as Vietnam, Thailand, Indonesia, Egypt, and Afghanistan. "In everything we do, we highlight the transformation of individuals and local communities," Roberts says.[2]

NorthWood's Six Measurement Points

The idea of transformation is such an important issue that Bob Roberts and NorthWood have developed a new scorecard for measuring their progress as a church. They do continue to count in traditional ways—they still tally financial offerings, worship attendance, and small-group involvement. But they place far more emphasis on certain measures of transformation. "A transformed life's supreme focus is to glorify God," says Roberts. Leaders at NorthWood believe transformation takes place in believers' lives by living out God's kingdom in the following three ways:

1. *Interactive relationship with God.* This involves worship, hearing God, and responding to God in obedience. Disciplines like Bible reading, prayer, private and corporate worship, and journaling are all part of a transformational walk with God.

2. *Transparent connections.* This involves interaction with other followers of Christ as they authentically encourage, instruct, and support one another. Typically this happens best in the small-group life of the church.

3. *Glocal impact* (a word that represents "global" and "local" combined). This involves using one's vocation not only to touch the community locally but also the world. For example, a team of educators and special needs specialists from NorthWood Church developed a special education curriculum for the entire nation of Vietnam. NorthWood's ten-member team then went to Vietnam to help Hanoi University educational officials implement the curriculum.

As individuals in churches manifest these transformations, they will make a lasting difference together, according to Roberts. He and NorthWood measure the differences as to how churches are progressing in these ways:

1. *Church multiplication.* Healthy churches strive for multiplication on every level—disciples, churches and clusters of churches. "All healthy organisms reproduce," says Roberts. "It is in their DNA to look beyond themselves to the next generation or the species dies."

2. *Community development.* The poor, the hungry, schools, businesses—must be different because our churches exist, Roberts believes. Jesus affirmed the need to care for those in need when he said, "For I was hungry and you gave Me something to eat; I was thirsty and you gave Me something to drink; I was a stranger and you took Me in . . ." (Matthew 25:35–36).

3. *Global engagement.* Roberts believes that what God told Abraham should also be said of churches today: "I will bless you . . . and all the peoples on earth will be blessed through you" (Genesis 12:2–3). Tonight many in the world will go to bed hungry, sick, uneducated, and without hope for the future. Glocalnet churches are helping improve and even rebuild infrastructures in countries. By working with international government leaders, Glocalnet church members are using their vocational skills to touch lives halfway around the globe, even in some of the most turbulent regions of the world.

Changing the Way Other Churches Measure

The rate of church planting seems to have soared in recent years across North America. With the move toward multiplying networks, we could see this trend continue for the next decade as well.

As church planters already know, this country is underchurched. The United States has far more church buildings than the number of McDonalds, Starbucks, and Dunkin' Donuts stores combined, giving the impression that there's a church facility on every corner and plenty of room for anyone who wants to take part. In reality, if the entire population of more than three hundred million Americas wanted to go to an established church,

The rate of church planting seems to have soared in recent years across North America.

including those that meet in storefronts, rented school facilities, and the like, more than half would be turned away, even if every church held three weekend services! That means we lack room for ninety-four million people. As it stands, one out of three houses or apartment units on your street would not have a place in worship this weekend. Table 12.1 shows the math.

> *As it stands, one out of three houses or apartment units on your street would not have a place in worship this weekend.*

Yet our focus here is not on seating capacity so much as on relational equity. That is, we're far less concerned with having a place to house worshipers (a comparatively easy problem to solve) as with lacking an environment full of trust to welcome such people. Most people will not connect with a church without a relational bridge that speaks their heart language. By heart language, we don't mean simply speak English to English-speakers and Hindi to immigrants of India.

Christians must measure their success along

> *Churches need just as much relational intelligence as linguistic skills.*

Table 12.1: Seating Capacity of U.S. Protestant Churches, If All Were Full[3]

240	average seating capacity per church
×300,000	number of churches
72,000,000	total number of seats
×3	three services per church
216,000,000	**total seating capacity of 216 million**
310,000,000	national population
− 216,000,000	minus seating capacity (at 3 services per church)
94,000,000	**94 million people to be turned away**

the spectrum of their willingness to communicate the Gospel to an inner-city New Yorker who grew up in an irreligious, alcoholic family—like someone did for Ed, leading to Ed's conversion to a life of following Jesus. Churches need just as much relational intelligence as linguistic skills. These interpersonal bridges need to happen in every culture, language group, and neighborhood across America.

These needs will be addressed only by tens of thousands of new churches in the United States. The only way that will take place is if more churches shift from individual church planting to a movement of church multiplication. So it is time for a new scorecard.

We believe a full-fledged church multiplication movement could happen in this country during our lifetime. Historically it's happened only once on these shores: the 1795–1810 church planting surge in frontier America we described in Chapter Four. But we're looking hard for evidence that one may develop soon.

When Ed served at the North American Mission Board several years ago, a team of church planting strategists returned from a meeting in London very excited about the prospect of rapidly reproducing church planting movements happening in this era. With an excitement that was contagious, they suggested that this was occurring in many places around the world, perhaps including the United States.

Ed, as well as others from his mission group, began the process of locating and reporting on movements that might be occurring in this country. They began to hear reports of movements in Colorado, California, Rhode Island, and Texas.

Ed contacted or visited each of these locations. Talking with the folks in Colorado, he said, "I hear you guys have a church planting movement." Their reply was curious. "No," they said, "We don't have a movement, but they do in California." So Ed called California and they said, "We don't have a movement, but you should call Texas." So Ed called Texas, and they said, "Nope. Try Colorado." The rumor was nothing more than an urban church legend. It was encouraging, elusive, and ultimately untrue.

The Holy Grail of Church Planting

Ed's search for the mysterious church planting movements began to feel a lot like looking for the Holy Grail in the Middle Ages. Everyone *knows* that it exists, and everyone *knows* someone who has seen it. But the Grail always ends up two villages away, and when you search two villages away, the treasure is another two villages away. Likewise, today many people seem to be hearing a buzz about a church planting movement, so everybody thinks there is one—but somewhere else.

At present there are thirty-four western industrialized democracies in the world, including the United States. Unfortunately no church planting movements currently exist among the majority peoples in those countries. However there are such movements among western settings (Cuba), in industrialized societies (China), in democracies (many in Central and South America), and among majority peoples (many in Asia and Africa).

Should we conclude that church planting movements cannot occur in today's western world? Or can real, explosive, exponential, Acts-like church multiplication happen in our corner of the world, just as it is happening in other places at this very moment?

In Chapter Four we introduced David Garrison, author of the groundbreaking book *Church Planting Movements* and one of the world's leading authorities on global church planting movements. As we said in Chapter Four, he defines a church planting movement as "a rapid and multiplicative increase of indigenous churches planting churches within a given people group or population segment." They are rapid and multiplicative in starting new churches because they plant quickly and produce exponential growth. Two churches becomes four, four becomes sixteen, and so on. And such movements are indigenous because they grow up from within, even if a missionary or planter acts as the initial catalyst. The Gospel almost always enters an area from the outside, but when it truly takes root, a movement blossoms from and within the locals.

This is markedly different from the "addition" model in which foreign missionary planters saturate an area with new church starts. In the individual planter model, churches get planted only when the church planter is heavily involved on a personal level, and it takes far longer to start any significant number of churches.

Comparing Overseas to North America

Drawing from Garrison's research, plus Ed's expertise on North American church planting, which included the research Ed did for Leadership Network, we want to consider what such a movement might look like if it took place in a North American context.

Looking over the Two-Thirds World—parts of Asia, Africa, and Latin America—where millions of people are coming to faith in Jesus Christ through the church planting movements, Garrison generalized something he named the ten "universal elements of a church planting movement." According to his research, these qualities do not appear to be limited to one geographical, cultural, or sociological sector of the world. They have been documented in relatively affluent and impoverished urban areas, as well as rural, pluralistic, Hindu, Buddhist, communist, Muslim, Roman Catholic, animistic, and even post-Christian secular contexts.

Ed then adapted Garrison's list for a western industrial democratized context like North America, as shown in the box on the following page.

There is obvious overlap between the two lists. Garrison's list is based on his study of actual events and therefore descriptive, whereas Ed's list is intentionally hypothetical. It must be so because there are no church planting movements to analyze in North

Movement Comparison of David Garrison and Ed Stetzer

A. *David Garrison's Universal Elements of a Church Planting Movement*

1. Prayer
2. Abundant Gospel sowing (focus on evangelism)
3. Intentional church planting
4. Scriptural authority
5. Local leadership
6. Lay leadership
7. Cell or house churches (structures that enable rapid multiplication)
8. Churches planting churches
9. Rapid reproduction
10. Healthy churches

B. *Ed Stetzer's Ten Marks of Movemental Christianity in the West*

1. Prayer
2. Intentionality of multiplication
3. Sacrifice
4. Reproducibility
5. Theological integrity
6. Incarnational ministry
7. Empowerment of God's people
8. Charitability in appreciating other models
9. Scalability
10. Holism in overall approach

America. Beyond that, Ed has some reservations as to whether church planting movements, as Garrison has defined them, will ever be found in western industrialized democracies, which lack some of the cultural factors found in the tribal world.

Obstacles to North American Church Multiplication

Certainly, no movement will take place apart from the work of the Holy Spirit, and none of the following speculation is to presume that the Spirit will blow where *we* please. Still, it does invite the question—why are faithful, Gospel-driven, Spirit-filled planters and pastors, who are prayerfully and evangelistically implementing elements of church planting movements in western indigenous populations, not seeing widescale results? We have perhaps seen pre-movements in the west, but why no breakthrough? Even as movements have been attempted, why haven't they thrived?

The answer may not fully lie in what the church is or isn't doing, but rather what the church has become in the West. Ed and David Garrison worked to think through some of these issues, and the following is adapted from a paper they presented at a 2008 conference named Exponential.[4] The following obstacles are more present in a context such as the United States than in other places around the world where church planting has occurred:

Institutionalization into a Noncommunal Culture

The term *institutionalization* is widely used in social theory to denote the process of embedding something—for example a concept, a social role, values, norms, or modes of behavior—within an organization, a social system, or a society until it becomes an established custom or normative in that system. Churches become institutionalized as they embed themselves in a society as an established norm within that society. The process they use to achieve this is both unconscious and conscious.

The unconscious part occurs as church members experience the socioeconomic uplift of the Gospel, which may occur within only one generation or may take place over several generations. As sociologists and historians have observed, the spread of Protestant churches often accompanies an elevation of both individuals and their families from poverty-inducing habits and helps re-create a culture where steady employment, consistent child rearing, education, and general social stability become the norm.

A byproduct of this socioeconomic lift is a predictable drift away from those who continue in a lifestyle outside of the faith. As Christians grow in their faith, they tend to separate themselves from unbelievers, the culture, the world, and the community at large.

Conscious institutionalization occurs when brush arbor meetings are institutionalized into brick-and-mortar buildings. Uncredentialed revival preachers give way to a demand for seminary-trained and, eventually, doctorate-enhanced pastoral leaders. Furthermore, as the institution grows, a church accumulates staff to meet a growing array of congregational needs, thereby making the congregation more and more internally self-sufficient and less cognizant of non-Christians with whom they might otherwise have redemptive contact and relationships.

In his book *Reinventing American Protestantism*, scholar Donald Miller described the shift presented by movements such as the Vineyard, Calvary Chapel, and others. Movements like the Vineyard were once multiplying exponentially but are now starting new churches at a rate of only 10 percent per year—an impressive velocity, but certainly a loss of exponential momentum as institutionalization takes root.

> *The institutionalizing of the church is essentially its immunization to an evangelistic impulse.*

The institutionalizing of the church is essentially its immunization to an evangelistic impulse.

Cultural Christianity

In many churches with otherwise good motivations, disciple-ship has been dumbed down to mean acclimating converts to the Christian subculture. Following what Richard Niebuhr described almost a hundred years ago in his classic book, *Christ and Culture*, many Christians follow a "Christ against culture" paradigm by allowing the excellent Christian publishing, radio programs, music, and so on to build a "Christian bubble" around us.[5]

The problem is that one can be fully immersed in the American Christian subculture and never know Christ personally. By simply identifying with that subculture, many people consider themselves to be his followers. The existence of such a Christian subculture creates a latent resistance to movemental Christianity in this country.

Western Christians have yet to find a biblically faithful way to be a good sort of "in the world" without being "*of* the world." A real breakout of church multiplication in America will be a movement of the people and by the people, but not of the culture and by the culture. During recent decades, our Christianity looks more like a colony or commune. We're like the colonial British living in India, inviting people to change and be imitators of our culture, rather than a group on mission to engage the outside world with the Gospel.

Ecclesionomics

Economics is another factor often overlooked in considering the absence of church multiplication movements in this country. Here the normal pathway of a church, as it becomes established, is to hire a pastor and fund a facility. These economic realities often create invisible economic incentives and disincentives to spiritual growth within those churches. Unchecked, the normal response by a church working hard to fund a pastor, facility, and other min-istry costs is to see new churches as competition. Sending your tithers and workers away appears counterintuitive. This potential reality becomes a huge disincentive for the traditional church paradigm, which impedes the development of movements.

Ironically, this economic barrier in the established church may become the very dynamic that will lead to the emergence of a church multiplication movement in this country. As mission-minded churches look to start new churches, but simply do not have the money to purchase property, buildings, and hire full-time staff, other methods may become more attractive. Missiological thinking will challenge churches to greater creativity in ministry than ever before. Using God's people to start many different smaller relationally based churches could become a very attractive economic alternative in a cash-strapped society.

Labor-Segmented Clergification

In a post-labor industrialized society, if I'm sick I go to my doctor, if I need legal help I go to my lawyer, and if I need automotive help I go to my mechanic. And if I want spiritual help, where do I go? To the clergy?

In this country, we have "clergified" ministry. We have somehow taught, wrongly so, that people who want help with spiritual things must go to the professionals. The underlying value: If you are not professional clergy, then you probably can't help. Unfortunately this labor segmentation disempowers ordinary people from being involved in church multiplication.

Much of this attitude is birthed from the western view of discipleship which requires a certain level of "maturity" before a person is allowed to lead in ministry. In an overseas church planting movement, leaders of a house church may be only one lesson ahead of the people they are teaching. Sure, this has dangers and we are aware of them, but we must find more ways to give permission sooner.

Jesus sets a model for us in how he raised up and sent out his disciples. He didn't sit them down for three years to soak up a lot of information, doing only little talks until they earned a certificate. Instead, in the middle of their training he sent them out to heal people, serve people, and love people just like he demonstrated by his own life. Rediscovering the pattern of Jesus would go a long way toward helping to facilitate a church multiplication movement.

Rediscovering the pattern of Jesus would go a long way toward helping to facilitate a church multiplication movement.

Indigenous Believers Not Functioning as Priests

Consolidating power and merely delegating responsibilities are sufficient ways to maintain a single community, but they are terrible ways to exponentially reproduce Christian community. Movements occur only when the disempowered are given the freedom and responsibility to lead, along with the accountability to make it happen.

In western culture, the clergification of the church has marginalized those that God has called to be members of the body of Christ. The disempowerment of the laity simultaneously satisfies and disturbs many pastors. They suffer frustration from not being able to get others to do the work of ministry *and* enjoy the sense of satisfaction that comes from ruling the roost. Such codependency is the death knell of movemental Christianity. Pastors can help themselves and help the members of their local churches by being more intentional about equipping people. Once the people take up their proper role in ministry, then the pastors are free to fulfill their own roles in equipping the saints for the work of ministry (see Ephesians 4:11–13). Granted, this can be a difficult transition to make, but it is a biblical one.

In the historic movements of Baptists and Methodists on the Western Frontier, and later Pentecostals in middle America, terms like "anointing" are frequently mentioned. If one felt the anointing and the community embraced the anointing, permission to step into ministerial roles was a rather simple process. Over time, this process has understandably become more complex, involving licensing, seminary training, credentialing, and lots of paperwork. However, are there validations of the priesthood of all believers who become unintentionally trampled in this routinization?

Currently, the closest thing to a church planting movement we have in the Western Hemisphere is found in Cuba, where two or three explosive church multiplication movements among Baptist and Pentecostal groups have occurred. But they are being jeopardized by professionalism. Church leaders in Cuba speak of some 100,000 people waiting for baptism. Why are they waiting? Because their pastors say that unless an ordained, recognized pastor baptizes them, they are not really baptized. A crude sacerdotalism is challenging the potential of a booming movement of several thousand churches because mature believers are not empowered to baptize new believers.

Miller's *Reinventing American Protestantism* looks back to this shift in the Vineyard and the Calvary Chapel communities in the 1970s and 1980s, where the prime movers were not formally trained people.[6] They had a new view of what it meant to be a pastor. Basically, if you were gifted, called, and anointed, you were ready to plant. Leaders were unleashed based on call and anointing, not education and credentialing. But something unfortunate has happened in the professionalization and the clergification of the western church that has impacted their movements, and they've lost much of that ethos.

When we minimize the priesthood of believers, we lose massive impact for the Gospel. The church's believers are to be *incarnational* priests, being the hands, feet, and heart of Christ to

True reproduction occurs when people are given permission to function as God has gifted and directed.

others, including to those who may not have heard God's plan of salvation. We must discover how to empower the *indigenous* laity of each church so that as they become believers, they can function in a priestly role themselves, bringing their own lost families and friends to Christ. True reproduction occurs when people are given permission to function as God has gifted and directed.

Lack of Intentional Evangelism Combined with Social Good

Without exception, the church planting movements in the Two-Thirds World that are experiencing exponential growth through conversions all bear the mark of intentionality in evangelism and multiplication. These are movements where intentionality is focused on training people to share their faith and holding them accountable to follow through on their training.

This just doesn't seem to be happening in America. If it is happening, it occurs most often in outmoded, nonindigenous ways or as a sales pitch for a particular gathering. No current western phenomenon of aggressive person-to-person relational evangelism is apparent, and we don't believe a church multiplication movement can happen in the West without it.

Instead, many churches are so focused on the biblical mandates to cultivate purity in the church that they have lost their outward focus on redeeming the lost. That is like divorcing Jesus' words about "repent and believe" from the "do good to others" teachings in the Sermon on the Mount.

Historical spiritual awakenings have always been accompanied by societal transformation. The movement we see among those self-labeled as "missional" is seeking to recapture the tie between the evangelistic and cultural mandates about which Ed often speaks, as based on Luke 4:16–21, which emphasizes that Jesus came to *serve*, and Luke 19:10, which emphasizes that Jesus came to *seek and save the lost*. The first is more of a cultural mandate as Jesus, in the earliest days of his ministry, was quoted in Isaiah 61 saying, "The Spirit of the Lord is on Me, because He has anointed Me to preach good news to the poor. He has sent Me to proclaim freedom to the captives and recovery of sight to the blind, to set free the oppressed, to proclaim the year of the Lord's favor" (Luke 4:18–19). Jesus gives his evangelistic mandate in Luke 19:10: "For the Son of Man has come to seek and to save the lost." Both perspectives are impulses for kingdom living and both should characterize why we plant churches.

A multiplying movement will result, with individual lives redeemed by the Gospel combined with the culture being impacted by God's kingdom. At a movement level, they are inseparable inevitabilities. But in today's iteration of missional church, we are witnessing a splintering of theology on numerous fronts which may actually hinder a church multiplication movement.

> *A multiplying movement will result, with individual lives redeemed by the Gospel combined with the culture being impacted by God's kingdom.*

Too often in the United States, discipleship means gaining knowledge. Elsewhere, it more often means social action. Our obedience to Christ's mandates has both a heavenly goal (glorify God) and an earthly implementation (salvation of the lost and redemption for the culture). If our hearts are passionate for Christ's agenda then we will avoid today's form of monasticism that replaces God as the center of our faith and substitutes with a focus on "me" and my own development. Church multiplication movements will readily follow churches whose hearts beat large with intentional evangelistic engagement as a result of societal change.

Lack of Intentional Reproduction

In the 1970s and 1980s, when Campus Crusade for Christ tried to create movemental momentum in personal evangelism, they saw thousands of people come to faith in Christ. But the missing piece for them was a lack of intentionality in planting churches for these new believers. The same situation has happened around the world. Many groups like Campus Crusade have reported that they cannot find a huge percentage of the people that they know they've led to Christ and discipled, especially those in underchurched countries. That's because they didn't have an ecclesiology or a strategy for intentional church planting.

Campus Crusade is now working to identify church planting strategists within their ranks and send them to their Best Practices Institute, which offers basic training in how to precipitate a church planting movement. In India, for example, they are working to take the effective evangelism that they do and link it with the intentional planting of reproducing churches. The difference is already noticeable.

YWAM (Youth with a Mission) began several years ago to couple their ministry work in India with intentional church planting. The result has been a proliferation of fruit that lasts. It is no surprise that organizations around the world including Campus Crusade are now becoming intentional about factoring new church starts into their remarkable evangelistic programs. Their large evangelistic outreach strategies are morphing into church planting strategies. They are taking the new tactic of intentionally moving people from their large events to small communities—in another word, churches.

Movements do not normally occur through large frameworks such as big budgets, big plans, big teams, or big organizations. Movemental Christianity does not seem to emerge from big-box programming. With large events and complex programming, it is a nearly impossible feat to accomplish.

Movements occur through small units that are readily reproducible.

Movements occur through small units that are readily reproducible. Those who want to see movements happen need to create simple structures that welcome reproducibility at every level. Being nimble and flexible is all important. Your challenge and ours is to test the usual systems and structures for their ability to reproduce and then resist the unnecessarily grandiose in favor of the reproducible.

Being nimble and flexible is all important.

Jesus' teaching about new wine fitting into old wineskins (see Matthew 9:16–17) must be rigorously applied to our structures. Structures must accommodate movements, not vice versa. Intentionally surveying, testing, and adjusting our structures for reproduction helps

Structures must accommodate movements, not vice versa.

to avoid crushing a movement under the weight of an organization. When God begins a multiplying movement, believers must value and work to strengthen the structures in a rapidly changing environment. In many cases, movements will break out of existing structures. If a congregation is intentional about the replication, then these movements will be celebrated. And what we celebrate, we duplicate and replicate. Celebrating multiplication guards us from allowing our existing structures to become bottlenecks rather than catalysts.

The Drift Toward Theological Bankruptcy

People sometimes ask about the danger of heresy spreading through church multiplication movements. The best antidote to potential heresy is to drive people deeply into the authority of the Word of God. Stories are told, often as a mask for not wanting any local competition for church growth, of rogue planters leading hordes of believers astray from orthodoxy. Church planting movements are usually found among people with robust beliefs, not generic belief systems. Churches wanting to be involved in transformative, movemental Christianity typically hold firm and passionate positions on biblical views.

Almost all movements have very strong integrated theological systems. In David Hesselgrave's *Dynamic Religious Movements*, he points out that the movements have a passion for their beliefs.[7] The way to create a church multiplication movement on this continent is not by deemphasizing belief systems. Rather, it is by enhancing the view that proper doctrine is the work of the all the saints, not just a special clergy classification.

In robust growing movements around the world, people respect and honor Scripture as God's Word in conjunction with a spiritual robustness of knowing God. And this knowledge of God, especially the soul-stirring and foot-moving immediacy of it, is something that has incredible effects when it is connected to the empowerment of God's people to minister and witness.

Defining the New Scorecard

We have identified the challenges and peeled back some of the hidden barriers to church multiplication movements in North America. Now let's talk about some prescriptions for positive advance. What is it going to take to see church multiplication movements take root in the west?

What is it going to take to see church multiplication movements take root in the west?

Our churches do not lack for programs and plans. But if you've tried everything available and nothing seems to be working in terms of building momentum for a movement of rapidly multiplying churches, you not only have a license to experiment but also an *obligation* to do so. We are in the midst of a missiological mystery here in the West.

We know God desires the multiplication of new communities of disciples but the question remains, "How does God desire to accomplish this here?" Toward the fulfillment of this vision, we can rejoice and keep trying to find what God wants to use and bless. We don't have to satisfy ourselves with the same approaches that have proven fruitless again and again. After all, the definition of insanity is to keep repeating what you have been doing while expecting to see different results.

If what we have been doing has not yielded fruit, then as you continue to pray, do not hesitate to innovate and adjust your methods. You just might find the key to the breakthrough that we all desire.

Let's review some of the obstacles to North American church multiplication identified in this chapter:

1. Institutionalization into a noncommunal culture
2. Cultural Christianity
3. Ecclesionomics
4. Labor-segmented clergification
5. Indigenous believers not functioning as priests
6. Lack of intentional reproduction
7. The drift toward theological bankruptcy

We believe these obstacles can all be overcome by

1. Abundant, fervent prayer—prayer that builds bridges between the lost and the God who seeks relationship with them.
2. Abundant, aggressive evangelism—evangelism that is exercised in every sector of society, not solely from the pulpit but within the marketplace, academy, neighborhood, and home.
3. Empowerment of the laity to be the people of God, a holy priesthood drawing the lost around them to new life in Christ.

4. Intentional evangelism and church planting—not leaving either to chance, but deliberately engaging every sector of society with multiplying new churches.

5. Biblically coherent, theological robustness—a theological commitment that is accessible and owned by every Christian because it is grounded in the faithful interpretation and application of the Word of God to the needs of the day.

Shifts like these call for a changing of the scorecard, but in order to see a radical move of God, radical change is needed. The Book of Acts shows that evangelism and church planting are the normal activity of normal believers filling the normal practice of starting normal churches. The question remains: Why isn't it normal for us here? What has separated us from our Christian brothers and sisters of the first century?

This separation might be due to our segmentation of discipleship from church planting, learning from replicating. Discipleship and church multiplication must be seen as both-and rather than either-or. Jesus invites his disciples to learn how to "fish for people" (Matthew 4:19) This isn't some magical formula; it's a promise to teach us how to usher people into the kingdom. Jesus' model was to be always fishing, always reaching out, always on the move, and, therefore, always engaging new people—new lost people. Jesus' example is intrusive and instructive. We've got to awaken that dynamic in the American church before it goes to sleep in a cocoon of self-focus.

North America does not need to be the only continent where the overall church is not growing nor where the majority of our churches have reached a plateau or are declining. Instead, all churches, whether new or old, can develop a new sense of scorecard, one marked

> *North America does not need to be the only continent where the overall church is not growing.*

by multiplying everything they do with their eyes ever focused on the Lord of the harvest and his call to "pray to the Lord of the harvest to send out workers into His harvest" (Matthew 9:38). Now, go and plant a movement, not just a church—a movement that has viral potential for multiplying the number of workers being deployed.

May God grant each reader discernment in how best to step forward to see multiplication occur as churches planted, the kingdom of God expanded, and lives changed by the Gospel of a powerful and loving God.

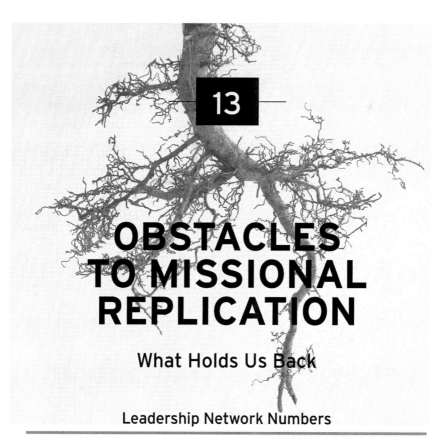

13

OBSTACLES TO MISSIONAL REPLICATION

What Holds Us Back

Leadership Network Numbers

A Google search on "church planting" produces over one million Web pages, suggesting that people are interested in church planting in a way not seen for many decades. However, a similar search on "church multiplication" generates only about 20 percent as many Internet hits, suggesting that fewer people are thinking about multiplication than addition.

"True success comes only when every generation continues to develop the next generation," observes John Maxwell, a best-selling author and former pastor.[1] Few churches demonstrate that reality better than East 91st Street Christian Church, which has been planting churches for decades. Its vision has stayed strong even through financial hard times and changes of pastors.

In the summer of 1924, the church that would eventually be named East 91st Street Christian Church held its first meeting under a tent on a street corner in Indianapolis, Indiana. (No, it wasn't yet on East 91st Street.) In 1951, when Russ Blowers began what became a forty-five-year ministry with the church, attendance on his first Sunday was eighty-five. The senior minister had a great vision for what God would do through this congregation. A year later the congregation sent out its first missionary. Soon enough it planted its first church. Ministry continued to expand, and during the 1980s the church purposed to plant twenty daughter churches in twenty years.

The church has welcomed several new senior ministers over recent years, but its vision for church planting—among many other ministries—has continued, all designed to "help all people become growing disciples of Jesus Christ." In 2008 the church started its fifty-first daughter church. It is now on a pathway to start fourteen more churches between 2009 and 2012. East 91st has relied on and built from an ethos and passion for planting new congregations. Its long-term dedication should serve as a catalyst for established churches and an inspiration to new churches that church planting can be done indefinitely if it represents your heart.

More Good Models Than Ever

It was a bit challenging to decide which illustration to use in starting this chapter. Our dilemma was not a lack of positive examples, but an abundance of them. We've tried to describe one or more heroes in each chapter. We hope you've found examples that relate to your context. If you're urban, for example, we hope you took note of Redeemer Presbyterian Church (Chapter Five) among others. If you're exploring house churches, we wanted you to know about Neil Cole's organic church movement (Chapter Eight), among others.

We've also profiled a bunch of church planting networks, such as NewThing (Chapter Seven) and Association of Related Churches (Chapter Nine). Each has a different strength. For example Acts 29 (Chapters Six and Eleven) has launched a degree-granting graduate program named Resurgence Training Center as part of a strategy for preparing leaders to plant a thousand churches in the United States.

A network we haven't introduced yet is Vision360, a city-centric church planting model. The vision is for church planters from a variety of denominations or networks to work together as one to reach a city. In Orlando, Florida, for example, Vision360 started twenty-five churches in less than four years with a total attendance of about seven thousand people. The Vision360 team provides a high level of care to each church planting family, including preassessment, assessment, training, coaching, mentoring, and resourcing in many forms, including financial.

To do all this, they've needed substantial funding. Steve Johnson, one of the founding partners of Vision360, who has previously planted many churches, has learned much about inviting successful business leaders to embrace their model. One example: they have four full-time people who work on Vision360 without a salary. They have huge vision and have brought many business leaders alongside it.

Other church planting networks have a dual focus, with good success both locally and globally. For example, since 1991 Grace Global Network has trained over four thousand church planters worldwide who have planted more than five thousand reproducing and multiplying churches, most overseas.

We didn't linger on many specific denominations in this book, but we could have. The nation's largest Protestant denomination, the North American Mission Board of the Southern Baptist Convention, is solidly behind church planting, both in the United States and Canada. The Assemblies of God is a good example of a major denomination with a strong emphasis on church planting, especially through their MX9 approach. For a midsize denomination, check out Converge Worldwide, a new denominational name that the Baptist General Conference adopted in 2008. For a smaller denomination, look at what the Missionary Church is doing with church planting.

Many leaders are way beyond basic gateway questions like "Why not just strengthen the churches we already have?" and "Don't we already have enough churches?" At all levels today, we're actually seeing examples of the multiplication that happened in Acts and what Paul instructed to be done in 2 Timothy 2:2—the training (and releasing) of others who train others who train others who train still others.

Church leaders are shifting focus from seating capacity to sending capacity.

Getting past the place where the highest value is the attendance figures from the previous Sunday is becoming normative, especially among pastors. Otherwise, you would not be reading this book! Church leaders like you are instead looking at how many people have yet to be reached, and are starting churches (among other things) to address that need. They're shifting focus from seating capacity to sending capacity.

Other Hurdles Remain

Even with all this good progress, several significant hurdles remain before missional multiplication takes off in the United States. Following are some thoughts of what has started to happen, but must continue at a higher and more widespread level.

1. Driving DNA Passion for Church Planting

People will need to consider church planting as one of their ministry's core values ("We glorify God by teaching the Bible, transforming the community and planting churches"). Church planting cannot be an afterthought, someone else's ministry, or a department. Churches will live, eat, and breathe it.

The widespread expectation that people will be sent out must become normal rather than exceptional. First-time planters need to assume and plan for the sending away of people. Movement leaders need to engender this attitude into the greater life of the church today. Pastors of established churches need to embrace it as a personal measure of their ministry. Church multiplication will become inherent in the DNA of our churches only as far as it is inherent in the DNA of our leaders.

> *Church multiplication will become inherent in the DNA of our churches only as far as it is inherent in the DNA of our leaders.*

2. New Measures of Success

More and more leaders will ask each other, "How many churches has your church has been involved in starting?" and "How many people have you deployed in mission and ministry?" and "What is your church's sending capacity?" Churches will always have a scorecard. A change of measures changes the current peer pressure and also creates positive peer pressure toward accomplishing the goal.

As in all instances, scorecards can either press toward the goal or become a source of pride or depression. The chest-thumping meetings where we compared our Sunday attendances with one another are beneath the calling

> *We replicate what we celebrate.*

to ministry. With our emphasis on a multiplication movement, a new scorecard will lend itself toward opening relationships and dialogue between church leaders. Let's cross the proverbial aisles to help those in varying denominations, networks, and methodologies to celebrate how God is multiplying churches. Then our members will do the same. We replicate what we celebrate.

3. More Roots in Historic Biblical Discipleship

Too often a church can't multiply its leaders because it has too few robust disciples. Instead it has lots of dependent believers who take a consumeristic approach to their faith and ultimately are shallow in character development. Multiplying churches are going to do a better job of disciple making. This is due to their determination to emphasize the transformation occurring in small communities and to simpler church structures that give more time to personal formation.

Modernity produced a discipleship model that is knowledge-based. If you could find Galatia on the map in the back of your Bible, then you must be a star student. But as we've known all along, and what is now blatantly obvious, basic spiritual information is important but not enough. Leadership multiplication is crucial. The need for a multiplication movement demands that we transform believers who are now in the sheep pen into leaders of new flocks.

4. Less Facility-Driven

Future churches will be less tied to the construction of buildings. The multisite movement is helping our culture accept the idea of "de-building" large church facilities. The average megachurch seating capacity is only fourteen hundred (median).[2] The average for all Protestant churches is 240.[3]

We think the small facility will get smaller. But more important, people's minds will more completely detach "facility" from "church." That shouldn't be too hard because it's not in the Bible. Nor is it as big a deal to the unchurched as we might imagine. Ed recently polled twelve hundred people, asking, "If you were considering visiting or joining a church, would knowing that the church does not meet in a traditional church building impact your decision?" Surprisingly, 73 percent said it made no difference. And whereas 19 percent said it would negatively affect their decision, another 6 percent believed that meeting in a nontraditional building was an asset for a church.

Churches will not cease from having facilities. But we can drop the hyperbolic reliance on the "if you build it, they will come" mentality. Multiplication movements are built on the principle of easily reproducible models, and facilities must follow suit.

5. Non-Anglo Leadership

Churches in the United States have heard that the growth hub of our faith is both south and east of us—such as South America, Africa, and Asia. Now that North American Christians are understanding the reality of God's movement in other churches around the world, however, it is time to for us to assume a position of learning from the global Christian community. We can learn much, for example, from the worldwide church planting movements I described in the previous chapter.

Here in the United States, the majority of church growth continues to come from immigrant and non-Anglo congregations. They may take a leadership role in this country's church multiplication movement because their congregations may be willing to multiply sooner and faster than others.

Speaking as two of the most white-skinned leaders you'll ever meet, we are looking forward to the multitude of lessons to be learned from our brothers and sisters leading multiplication movements in far-flung places around the world.

6. Less Permanency

To many of us, the idea of churches forming, flourishing, and then going away, all somewhat quickly, seems to be a bad thing. We need to get a sense that God's people will last for eternity, but our facilities can be far less permanent. In fact, lots of churches died thirty years ago, but no one turned out the lights. The building serves as the respirator for churches on life support.

In the near future, they'll come, they'll go, and we'll all be aware that God used them. Saints persevere, but their institutions and facilities are temporary. As new congregations are formed in the multiplying movements, we will view church facilities as kingdom

Church buildings are like an inheritance to pass along rather than a living trust to keep.

assets. Church buildings are like an inheritance to pass along rather than a living trust to keep.

7. Multiple Pacesetters

"Historically all movements have begun because of the charismatic efforts of one lone individual who touched a nerve among a host of people. Who will step up to be that person?" That's what our friend Bill Easum advised us. He's a prolific writer and coauthor of *Ten Most Common Mistakes Made by New Church Starts.*[4]

We think we're seeing multiple people step up, all sharing the same stage. Part of what we wanted to do in this book is to introduce network leaders to many other people and networks that they might not know about. Lots of good things are happening—but for a church multiplication movement to happen, the small stream has to become an unstoppable rushing river. And we think that you are ready to begin guiding people down the rapids.

What Holds Us Back

Church planting is hot today, and in many ways denominations are not. We fear that some people are doing the network thing because it's cool, and they're perhaps more excited about their network than about the idea of reaching lost people. So a word of caution: if you're in it because it's trendy or because you are against your last experience, then revisit Acts 8 and 18.

In Acts 8, God is moving so powerfully in Samaria through Philip that Peter and John come to help in the citywide awakening. But Simon the Sorcerer is immature in his understanding of what is happening and simply wants a touch of the power he sees. Seeing that Simon is in it only because it's the latest spiritual fad, Peter gives him a sharp rebuke. We need to hold our lives up against Simon and be tested by the Spirit. Is it for personal gain or God's glory that we are ready to start a movement of churches?

Acts 18 gives us a different scenario. In it, Apollos is traveling around Ephesus making an impact for the way of the Lord. But there are still places in his understanding that are not fully formed. When invited by Priscilla and Aquila to learn the fuller understanding of the Gospel, he humbles himself to their teaching. He is not in it for vainglory but for the spiritual impact of the city. Consequently, he is becomes a great help to those coming into the kingdom of God.

Choosing to be Apollos instead of Simon will allow you to become a movement leader. Public power will make you famous for a while, but steady gospel transformation will make you useful for a lifetime. Simon is never mentioned again in the scriptures but Apollos becomes a leader of the church.

If more people can decide to learn what God is up to in church planting movements, then we may be blessed to see them populate the continent in the next decade. We hope you will learn to do small well, to create cultures of permission-giving for God's people, and to multiply everything. Then we'll move from church starting (a broad category that includes church splits) to church planting

> *If more people can decide to learn what God is up to in church planting movements, then we may be blessed to see them populate the continent in the next decade.*

(focused on reaching lost people) to church multiplication (people self-initiating to go out into the harvest, and then passing to them a heart for multiplication).

If so, then a church planting movement might be closer than we think. And the kingdom of God will take root into more lives than we could have ever dreamt or imagined.

14

CONCLUSION

Solving the Toughest Challenges

This book has identified an enormous problem in the way North American Christians approach church planting. It has assumed that the number of churches in existence is woefully short of what is necessary to give every American the opportunity to meet followers of Christ who are like them and can model new life in Jesus Christ, helping them to find spiritual rebirth. It has proposed a new perspective on church planting— one that "thinks" multiplication rather than addition. A trajectory that will dramatically increase the number of new churches started each year. A culture in which every church sees replication as normal, healthy, desirable, and attainable. We want to see multiplication become not just something to which we aspire but something that is preferable and normative. In other

> *We are advocating a church multiplication movement.*

words, we are advocating a church multiplication movement, which we have defined as an exponential rate of birthing new churches, all of which engage lost people and replicate themselves through even more new churches.

Conventional wisdom says that any denomination that doesn't plant 3 percent new churches per year will lose ground. The 3 percent target is a minimum that must be reached simply to maintain the current size of a denomination due to church closings, which average 3 percent annually for the typical denomination.

We are delighted that many denominations have increased their emphasis on church planting, some now achieving growth of 1 percent annually, others 2 percent, and still others 3 percent. Though they are very few, some are even launching more than 3 percent each year. We're thankful for the prayers and Scripture-based church planting books, conferences, research projects, and conversations that have led to this uptick.

Likewise, a handful of nondenominational quarters have become church-planting enthusiasts, more so than at any time in at least a hundred years. Churches are creating and enlarging internship programs that are designed to raise up and mentor future church planters. Seminaries and Christian colleges have formed church planting centers to do likewise. Parachurch groups have developed church planting "boot camps" and assessment processes designed to develop more and better church planters. Spontaneous networking is occurring more frequently around church planting than probably any of us is aware.

But perhaps the greatest development is that churches are more passionate about planting churches than we have seen since the end of the nineteenth century. The new millennium seems to have birthed a new ethos within the church of North America. Perhaps we have regained what was lost but still active in many other places around the world. We are watching a renaissance of church planting that is occurring naturally in churches, organically through new networks, and technologically through online tribal communities of church leaders.

These are great things, but they're only the beginning of what needs to happen. The old image of "charging with a water pistol" is not enough. Shortly after John Bunyan wrote his famous *Pilgrim's Progress*, he penned a lesser known novel, *The Holy War*. Its story centers on the city of Mansoul, its capture by Diabolus, and its freedom delivered by Prince Emmanuel. In the end, Prince Emmanuel tells the freed people, "You shall see your Prince show himself in the field; for we must make this second assault upon this tyrant Diabolus, and then Emmanuel comes."[1]

Merely tweaking our current approaches to church will never be enough. To see a multiplying church planting movement, we will have to move from water pistol rhetoric to actually advancing against the gates of Hades with "Prince Emmanuel" leading our way. We believe it is beginning among many of those reading this book.

> *To see a multiplying church planting movement, we will have to move from water pistol rhetoric to actually advancing against the gates of Hades with "Prince Emmanuel" leading our way.*

We Need to Take Another Approach

If a church multiplication movement is to happen in the United States, it is highly unlikely to come from our current structures and systems, and not even from our more vigorous approaches to church planting in recent years. If we carry our current methods and approaches to their logical end, maybe we could push the current system harder to generate a few more churches, but it is already close to capacity. We already have almost all the church planting that our current money can buy and our current systems can support.

Instead, we need to imagine a different world, one that begins with an end in mind. The desired goal is to see lost people find new life through Jesus Christ—not at the rate at which the general population is growing (which isn't even happening), not even at a rate that gains respectable ground, but at a velocity and intensity that is nothing short of explosively supernatural. Isn't that what Jesus described in numerous places, from "making disciples of *all* nations" (Matthew 28:19; emphasis added)? Isn't this what his parable is about of mustard seed growth from seed to "largest" plant and tree (Matthew 13:31–32)? Isn't he inviting us to pray that God's "will be done on earth as it is in heaven" (Matthew 6:10)? Seriously, what would it be like if your community, city, state, and country were places where the majority of people were eager to do God's will in the same way it's done in heaven?

> *The desired goal is to see lost people find new life through Jesus Christ at a velocity and intensity that is nothing short of explosively supernatural.*

You've perhaps heard about genuine Great Awakenings and revivals that happened on this continent. Can you imagine a scenario where another Great Awakening occurs locally in your lifetime? Envision it on a scale of millions. Picture spiritual life transformations in every city among Americans who have spiritual curiosities and longings, but currently lack a personal relationship with a believer bent on multiplication. We should get a picture of connecting every unbeliever with someone who puts God first in their life to act as the bridge that might connect them with a multiplying church in their community. Then, as new believers are birthed into the kingdom, they would have the natural inclination toward multiplication instead of making only periodic additions to the church.

We need a new story for that to happen. A multiplication story. That's what *Viral Churches* is about. We need to give church planters permission to live within that story and the encouragement to take great risks of faith in learning how to be multipliers and permission-giving releasers. We need to encourage denominational leaders to apply their theology to a new multiplication paradigm, both to validate and bless it—and perhaps also to take some arrows that otherwise would hit the backs of their church planters.

Evangelism

We began this book with the understanding that church planting and evangelism are inseparably linked. Remember, we want
to move from missionary journeys to church planting journeys.
In other words, our goal is not just to meet and evangelize; we
must congregationalize. The Great Commission is not just a call
to "make disciples" but
to "baptize." In Acts
and elsewhere, it is clear
that baptism means
incorporation into a
worshipping commu-
nity with accountability
and boundaries (such as
Acts 2:41–47). The only way to be truly sure you are increasing
the number of Christians in a town is to increase the number of
churches.

> *The only way to be truly sure*
> *you are increasing the number of*
> *Christians in a town is to increase*
> *the number of churches.*

There are certainly people who start churches for reasons other
than evangelism: a church splits, a church started to feed a leader's
ego or need for control, a church started to be a more convenient
location for members of the sending church, and so on. We believe
Jesus' teaching on leaving ninety-nine sheep to find the one lost
sheep (Luke 15:1–7) is one of many examples that affirm a heart-
felt concern for people's brokenness and lostness. Jesus explicitly
modeled such compassion and care, affirming that the reason he
came to earth was "to seek and to save the lost" (Luke 19:10).

In many ways, church planting has become what other
approaches once were. For example, many outreach-minded campus
ministries are now new church plants near or on campuses. Many
large evangelistic meetings are now large launch services in new
churches. Likewise, as other methodologies have lost some of their
effectiveness, new church planting has come in as a substitute.

However, if the multiplication of church planting is to become
truly movemental, it will require an evangelistic intensity that is
still not widespread or deep enough. In most cases, the majority of

new attendees at new churches are still believers—either transfers from other churches or dropouts from previous churches. To truly shift to a movement, church plants—and the people who are part of such plants—must make intentional evangelism a defining and ongoing aspect of their new church.

Enthusiasm

In both of our denominations (and in many others), church planting here in the United States has moved only in recent decades away from being second class. Sometimes it's even been the red-headed stepchild of pastoral ministry. Planting was an uncommon calling. It was affirmed as biblical and effective, but few were doing it. For most of the twentieth century, church planting was definitely not the socially affirmed route for the "proper" people in ministry. In some denominations, it was not uncommon that the people planting churches were the ones who could not get "real jobs" at established churches.

Things have certainly changed in the last five years. A recent conference at one of the largest seminaries in the nation expressed concern that so many of the best and brightest were going into church planting that few were left to lead struggling established churches. That's quite a shift. One conference filled with church planters recently had a main session entitled, "Church Planting Is for Wimps: Try Revitalizing a Church." That's quite a change! Today, with church planting as a preferred ministry option for so many, sometimes the unprepared or the ill equipped have been swept up in the enthusiasm.

With this new wave of enthusiasm comes questions and opportunities. The questions are clear: is church planting growing because the traditional church is so unattractive? Are pastors wanting to do something that is easier (planting or birthing a baby) versus harder (revitalization or raising the dead)?

The opportunities are not nearly as clear. Sure, we can see where new churches are needed simply based on the demographics of church membership versus population. But the statistics of a city never fully communicate the opportunities awaiting a new church. Behind the numbers, we always find the lives of the people. They are the opportunity awaiting the church planter—watching lives transformed by the Gospel so the kingdom of God takes hold of a city.

> *The motivation must be that the name and fame of God would be more widely known.*

For church planting to truly become a movement of multiplication, it will need to move from being "the next big thing" to a passionate pursuit of the lost that leads to life transformation. The motivation cannot be to build a church you've always wanted. It must be that the name and fame of God would be more widely known.

Multiplication

This book can be summarized in two words: multiply everything. That means to build environments where disciples, leader groups and churches spend most of their time reproducing themselves, and to use structures that readily lend to being replicated. That perspective also

> *This book can be summarized in two words: multiply everything.*

involves a huge commitment to permission giving, empowerment, risk taking, and innovation. To maintain something is far easier than to train someone else to do it, and also to instill in that person the heart and skill to train yet others.

New Success Measures

The cultural qualities described in the previous section will lead to a shift in how pastors and church leaders measure success.

American culture says size is the measure of success, and many churches buy that definition. American churches have taken hold of Wall Street's measures of big and Hollywood's measure of glamour to determine the worth of our churches. Or they disavow them—but usually without offering an alternative.

The better option is to develop new benchmarks, such as a more organic mind-set that focuses on abundance versus size. In agricultural terms, farmers sows lots of seeds with the mind-set that they will reap more than they sow. As our friend Glenn Smith of New Church Initiatives told us, "Church planters that I've spoken with outside the U.S. have this abundance mind-set. They seem to focus more on the abundance of churches than on the size of each church. Then they expect their church plants to reproduce quickly." Perhaps we need to think more like farmers, hungering for the orchard that we're helping to plant to become wildly out of control. "Until this shift takes place we will never see a western movement except by a dramatic miracle of God. And even if he did this despite us, I think our reaction would be to control and contain it," Smith cautions.

Although we have both served on staff of megachurches, we're quick to affirm loudly that something small can usually reproduce more rapidly than something big. If a church of twenty people plants just one church of twenty each year, and if each of those churches plants just one church of twenty each year, and each of those likewise follow the cycle of planting one church per year, then in twenty years the original church would have multiplied into more than ten million people. That's the power of multiplication (see Table 14.1).

Deep Spirituality

Our friend Wayne Cordeiro, introduced in Chapter Nine, is yet another great role model of someone who not only plants individual churches, but who has developed an effective church planting network as well—one that has planted to date more than

Table 14.1: Comparison of a Twenty-Person Church That Adds Versus a Church That Multiplies

Year	Addition		Multiplication	
	Number of Churches	Number of People	Number of Churches	Number of People
1	1	20	1	20
2	2	40	2	40
3	3	60	4	80
4	4	80	8	160
5	5	100	16	320
6	6	120	32	640
7	7	140	64	1,280
8	8	160	128	2,560
9	9	180	256	5120
10	10	200	512	10,240
11	11	220	1,024	20,480
12	12	240	2,048	40,960
13	13	260	4,096	81,920
14	14	280	8,192	163,840
15	15	300	16,384	327,680
16	16	320	32,768	655,360
17	17	340	65,536	1,310,720
18	18	360	121,072	2,621,440
19	19	380	262,144	5,240,880
20	20	400	524,288	10,485,760

two hundred churches around the Pacific Rim. Cordeiro has a favorite saying that we wholeheartedly support: "We teach what we know, but we reproduce what we are."[2] This concept is especially applicable to the world of church planting. In fact, Cordeiro often conducts

> "We teach what we know, but we reproduce what we are."
>
> —WAYNE CORDEIRO

training for pastors of new churches, and he finds they mostly appreciate his emphasis on developing a solid devotional life. Why? If you don't practice the idea of being a self-feeder, doing so on the spiritual resource of God's Word, then at some point you begin running on empty.

Wayne Cordeiro had to learn this message the hard way. He had been in ministry for thirty years, and ten years after founding what is now the largest church in Hawaii, he found himself depleted, burned out, and leading on empty. Cordeiro took a season out of his growing ministry to recharge and refocus on what was truly important. He was able to get back in touch with his life, get back in proper balance, and reenergize his spirit through Christ in a way that propelled him forward to greater levels of service. More significant is that he learned to cultivate the character and strength of Christ in new ways for his own life, and then to replicate those practices throughout his congregation.[3] Too much of church planting today is more of an entrepreneurial quest than a spiritual experience. It's driven by leadership, which can be good, but not if the leader's prayer and spiritual devotion is running on empty. Too many church planters are weak as prayer warriors. They would honor God more by strengthening their inner person, and then leading from the vantage point of those spiritual disciplines and emotional health.[4]

Where Will You Go from Here?

The first few minutes of the movie *Saving Private Ryan* are incredibly painful to watch. The Americans have landed on the beach. Captain Miller (Tom Hanks) sees an opening for his men. It offers protection on the other side, a foothold that can lead to victory—if they can get through. "That's the route," he announces and immediately sends six men through the gap. They are brutally killed. The sergeant, who is more experienced, warns Miller with a stern look, "That's a ... shooting gallery, Captain," but Miller responds resolutely, "That's the route." Miller then commands another group of six: "Go." They obey and are likewise brutally cut down. Miller turns to the next six and says, "It's the only way … you're next." The third group loses several lives but finally breaks through the German lines.

It is a hard scene to watch. Many people close their eyes, unable to stomach the harsh realities of combat. Yet many military veterans hailed the movie for how well it depicted the reality of what became the turning point in World War II.

That mix of risk, boldness, bravery, and persistence is what church planting has looked like for many past decades. Planters and their teams, unprepared for the challenges ahead, quickly charged into "harvest fields" that became "killing fields." They were enthusiastic but only a few met success. They were excited for the task but they were not ready to face the realities of church planting.

Ed's experience as a church planter paralleled the intensity of D-Day's vital gains at the cost of great loss. When Ed came to Buffalo to plant his first church, eight people also began other churches. All possessed great faith, enthusiasm, and bravery. Yet twenty years later, only one of the churches remain, and four of the eight have left the ministry, their marriage, and the faith. Ouch.

The wonderful good news—the facts that this book has documented—is that the past two decades have produced radical changes in how churches are planted. Not only has survivability dramatically increased, both for the planter's personal life and for the new churches formed, but church leaders have learned something even more important for the long run: to replicate themselves. Indeed, an embryo church multiplication movement is undeniably forming in many quarters of the country. It is marked by churches that birth other churches which, in turn, birth even more churches. Our hope and prayer is that this book will equip those church multiplication leaders and encourage thousands of others to join them.

As a result, new images are emerging for what the state of U.S. church multiplication today and tomorrow. We've used many pictures in this book, all designed to replace addition with multiplication as the dominant metaphor. These images started with the viral metaphor of the book's title. In-text analogies ranged from planting orchards (rather than individual trees) to expanding a sole Walmart checkout line to a whole new checkout system. All are intended to emphasize the difference between one versus many, adding versus multiplication.

A theologian, educator, and social critic named Ivan Illich was once asked if societal change would happen best through revolution or reform. He responded that it was neither—not if you desired long-term change. Rather, he said that we need to tell an "alternative story" that draws others because of its irresistible nature.the pages of this book, we have tried to tell an alternative story, one where everyone in the church, both leaders and congregation, see self-multiplication as desirable and normal. In fact, we argued from Scripture that this is nothing short of Jesus' calling and plan. It is our hope you have been drawn in by the telling and that you might join Jesus on his mission.

We believe the church matters to the mission of God. The church is not the center of God's plan. Jesus is. But the church is central to God's plan. And we look forward to the day when this alternative story is a present reality and new churches are literally being multiplied in number across North America and

How to Begin Your Church Multiplication Future Today

- What if every reader of this book seriously dealt with these questions: How am I replicating myself through other leaders? How am I not doing so? What do I need to *personally* change about my leadership style in order to raise up others?
- What if all churches were to encourage their youth to do two years of service in a church plant? What if it became normal

and expected, as in some other religions, that all Christian youth will do two years of missionary service between high school and college?

- What if every seminary were to expose its students to a vibrant church plant for three months of their seminary experience?

- What if the standard way that everyone described their church was to list how many churches they've planted? What if "number of churches we've birthed" became more important than "number of people attending our worship services"?

- What if churches with more resources gave more money away to church planting than the amount they use to maintain their buildings and programs?

- What if all church members saw themselves as church planting missionaries to family, friends, coworkers, and neighbors?

- What if the accepted time for churches to plant new churches became weeks or months rather than years?

ACKNOWLEDGMENTS

Church history begins with the story of a handful of Jesus' disciples who became church planters. Those churches planted other churches and sent out apostolic missionaries to start even more churches. Two thousand years later, our lives were each touched by a church in that string.

In that regard, we stand on a lot of great shoulders. We name several dozen such people in this book, but there are many more that we didn't have room to discuss. We especially want to commend Bob Logan, whose materials were highly formative for each of us; and church planters who personally mentored each of us— Mark Terry and David Hesselgrave for Ed, and Forrest Garrard, Carl George, and Dale Galloway for Warren.

We also have bosses who have supported and blessed us in writing this book—Thom Rainer for Ed, and Tom Wilson and Dave Travis for Warren. Special thanks also to Leadership Network for financially funding the original research that led to this book.

We also have great support staff who have assisted us in our writing. Ed heaps praise on Caleb Crider, Lizette Beard, Shirley Cross, and Phillip Connor. Warren heaps even more praise on Stephanie Plagens, Bonnie Randle, and Cynthia Beal. Bonnie in particular did a lot of groundwork and correspondence to help bring this book to completion.

We have several good friends who read an early draft and offered helpful and constructive feedback. They include Michelle

Bird, John Bishop, Joe Hernandez, Kep James, John Soper, Linda Stanley, Dan Morgan, Philip Nation, Dino Senesi, and J. Allen Thompson.

Our thanks finally to the editorial team that assisted us: Mark Sweeney and Greg Ligon from Leadership Network, and Sheryl Fullerton and Joanne Clapp Fullagar from Jossey-Bass.

Most of all, we're thankful for the dozens of church network leaders who allowed us to interview, study, and watch them—and then to tell their very exciting stories in this book. Many of them gave us great ideas for illustrations in the book, such as Glenn Smith, who made several editorial contributions to the book, but most of all reminded us that a church of twenty people can reach ten million people in twenty years—if it has the DNA of multiplication (see Table 14.1 in Chapter Fourteen).

APPENDIX

List of Churches and Networks Cited

Church or Network Name	City	State	Pastor or Leader	E-mail or Web site
Acts 29	Seattle	WA	Scott Thomas	www.a29.org
Association of Related Churches	Baton Rouge	LA	Billy Hornsby	www.relatedchurches.com
Bay Area Fellowship	Corpus Christi	TX	Bil Cornelius	www.bayareafellowship.com
Christ the King Community Church	Mt. Vernon	WA	Dave Browning	www.ctkonline.com
Church Multiplication Associates	Signal Hill	CA	Neil Cole	www.cmaresources.org
Church Resource Ministries	Anaheim	CA	n/a	www.crmleaders.org
Discipling a Whole Nation (DAWN)	Orlando	FL	n/a	www.dawnministries.org
East 91st Street Christian Church	Indianapolis	IN	Derek Duncan	www.east91st.org
First Baptist Church Hendersonville	Hendersonville	TN	Bruce Chesser	www.firstbaptist hendersonville.com
Glocalnet	Keller	TX	Bob Roberts	www.glocal.net
Grace Global Network	Estero	FL	Greg Kapas	www.graceglobalnetwork.org
Griffith Coaching	Centennial	CO	Jim Griffith	www.griffithcoaching.com
Imagine Fellowship	San Antonio	TX	Kevin Joyce	www.imaginefellowship.org
Kairos Church Planting	Portland	OR	Stan Granberg	www.kairoschurchplanting.org

Lexington Community Church	Lexington	NC	Eric Disher	www.safe-place.org
Mars Hill Church	Seattle	WA	Mark Driscoll	www.marshillchurch.org
New Church Initiatives	Sugarland	TX	Glenn Smith	www.newchurchinitiatives.org
New Hope Community Church	Honolulu	HI	Wayne Cordeiro	www.enewhope.org
NewThing Network	Naperville	IL	Jon Ferguson	www.newthing.org
NorthWood Church	Keller	TX	Bob Roberts	www.northwoodchurch.org
Perimeter Church	Duluth	GA	Randy Pope	www.perimeter.org
Seattle Church Planting	Bothell	WA	Gary Irby	www.seattlechurchplanting.com
Sovereign Grace Ministries	Gaithersburg	MD	C. J. Mahaney	www.sovgracemin.org
Stadia, East Region	Johnson City	TN	Tom Jones	www.stadia.cc
Stadia, West Region	Rocklin	CA	Marcus Bigelo	www.stadia.cc
Vision 360 Detroit	Troy	MI	Mike Harris	www.vision360detroit.org

NOTES

1. Introduction

1. Most hard statistics in this book will appear at the opening of each chapter under the heading "Leadership Network Numbers." The majority come from research that Leadership Network commissioned, some of which Leadership Network itself did, some of which Leadership Network outsourced, and some of which Leadership Network compiled but which was conducted or reported initially by other organizations. Further, a small amount of the data has no formal association with Leadership Network, such as U.S. Census Bureau statistics. The clearest and most unobtrusive way of bringing clarity to all these diverse sources is to attach an endnote to many of them.

2. Bird, Warren. "More Churches Opened Than Closed in 2006." *Rev Magazine* (July–Aug. 2007): 68.

3. From the internal Leadership Network study available in summary form only as a free download named *State of Church Planting U.S.A.*, available from www.leadnet.org.

2. Church Planting

1. This is from Joel Rainey's doctoral dissertation as reported in the internal Leadership Network study, *State of Church Planting USA*, available from www.leadnet.org.
2. This is from the Leadership Network study, *State of Church Planting USA*, along with data from the U.S. Census Bureau.
3. Wagner, C. Peter. *Church Planting for a Greater Harvest* (Ventura, CA: Regal Books, 1990): 11. Also stated in Wagner, C. Peter. *Strategies for Growth* (Ventura, CA: Regal Books, 1987): 168.
4. Only God knows the precise numbers! There are several reasons why. Some church planting groups are so organic that they simply don't keep track, and so the best they can do is estimate. A bigger problem is the danger of counting the same church two or more times. For example, suppose a new church is birthed through a cooperative venture of a sponsor church, a denomination, and a church planting network. Perhaps all of them will report that same church in their tally of new churches. Another example is a new church not reporting its affiliation with a denomination but the denomination reporting that church as one of its new church plants.
5. Stetzer, Ed, and David Putman. *Breaking the Missional Code: Your Church Can Become a Missionary in Your Community* (Nashville, TN: B & H Academic, 2006): 68.
6. Stafford, Tim. "Go and Plant Churches of All Peoples: Crusades and Personal Witnessing Are No Longer the Cutting Edge of Evangelism." *Christianity Today* (Sept. 2007): Vol. 51, p. 9.
7. "Churches Die with Dignity." *Christianity Today* (Jan. 1991): Vol. 36.
8. Meacham, Jon. *"The Global Elite: The Story of Power."* Available from www.newsweek.com/id/176300/page/1. Jan. 2009.

3. Growth by Multiplication

1. From Leadership Network study, *State of Church Planting USA*, available from www.leadnet.org.
2. Complete findings are available in the free download titled *FACT2008* from Hartford Institute for Religion Research, www.hartfordinstitute.org.
3. The ministry is named Winning the Second Billion Together. Its Web site is www.billionsoul.org. The specific conference is named Synergize and can be linked from that Web site.
4. Crouch, Andy. "Thou Shalt Be Cool." *Christianity Today* (Mar. 2002): Vol. 46.

4. New Players

1. Farmer, Jeffrey C. "Church Planting Sponsorship" (Ph.D. diss., New Orleans Baptist Theological Seminary, 2007). His findings are based on survey responses from 309 Southern Baptist churches that sponsored a new church in 1999; Farmer conducted his survey in 2006.
2. From Leadership Network study, *State of Church Planting USA*, available from www.leadnet.org.
3. Ibid.
4. Hatch, Nathan O., *The Democratization of American Christianity* (New Haven and London: Yale University Press, 1989): 30.
5. Goodykoontz, Colin Brummitt. *Home Missions on the American Frontier: With Particular Reference to the American Home Missionary Society* (Caldwell, ID: The Caxton Printers, 1939): 411–412.
6. Gaustad, Edwin Scott. *Historical Atlas of Religion in America* (New York: Harper and Row, 1962): 55. And Braun, Neil. *Laity Mobilized: Reflections on Church Growth in Japan and Other Lands* (Grand Rapids, MI: Eerdmans, 1971): 55.
7. Finke, Roger, and Rodney Stark. *The Churching of America: Winners and Losers in Our Religious Economy* (New Brunswick, NJ: Rutgers University Press, 1992).

8. Garrison, David. *Church Planting Movements; How God Is Redeeming a Lost World* (Richmond, VA: Wigtake Resources, 2003).

9. Ibid., p. 8.

10. For example, see Latourette, Kenneth Scott. *A History of the Expansion of Christianity, Vol. IV, The Great Century: Europe and the United States, 1815 A.D. to 1914 A.D.* (New York: Harper and Row, 1969).

11. Roger and Stark, *The Churching of America*, 73.

12. Goodykoontz, *Home Missions on the American Frontier*, 161–162.

13. Sanders, J. Oswald. *Spiritual Leadership: Principles of Excellence for Every Believer* (Moody, 2007): 119.

14. Phares, Ross. *Bible in Pocket, Gun in Hand* (Lincoln: University of Nebraska Press, 1971): 120.

15. Phares, *Bible in Pocket*, 165.

16. St. Amant, Penrose. "Frontier, Baptists and the American." In *Encyclopedia of Southern Baptists* (Nashville, TN: Broadman Press, 1982): 511.

17. Shurden, William B. "Associationalism Among the Baptists, 1707–1814" (Ph.D. diss., New Orleans Baptist Theological Seminary, 1967): 169.

18. One author who repeatedly uses that term is Sweet, William Warren. *Religion on the American Frontier, 1783–1840. Vol. IV, The Methodists* (Chicago: The University of Chicago Press, 1946).

19. Sweet, *Religion on the American Frontier*, footnote on page 40.

20. Sweet, *Religion on the American Frontier*, 39.

21. McBeth, H. Leon. *The Baptist Heritage* (Nashville, TN: Broadman Press, 1987): 368.

22. Finke and Stark, *The Churching of America*, 78.

23. Phares, *Bible in Pocket, Gun in Hand*, 15.

24. Sweet, *Religion on the American Frontier*, 54.

25. Allen, Judson Boyce. "Westward Expansion, Southern Baptist." In *Encyclopedia of Southern Baptists* (Nashville, TN: Broadman Press, 1982): 1490.

26. Thumma, Scott, and Dave Travis. *Beyond Megachurch Myths: What We Can Learn from America's Largest Churches* (San Francisco: Jossey-Bass, 2007).
27. Carol Wimber, *Back to Our Roots: Stories of the Vineyard, Doin' the Stuff*. DVD, 2006.
28. The Web site for the International Pentecostal Holiness Church is www.iphc.org/. The denomination's church planting Web site is http://evusa.iphc.org/chrplant.html.
29. Surratt, Geoff, Greg Ligon, and Warren Bird. *Multi-Site Church Revolution* (Grand Rapids, MI: Zondervan, 2006): 39–40, 154–156; Surratt, Geoff, Greg Ligon, and Warren Bird. *Multi-Site Church Roadtrip* (Grand Rapids, MI: Zondervan, 2009): 129–134.
30. Surratt, Ligon, Bird, *Multi-Site Church Revolution*, 154.
31. Surratt, Ligon, Bird, *Multi-Site Church Revolution*, 40.
32. Keener, Ron. "The CE Interview: Dave Browning" (Aug. 2009): 12–13.

5. Kingdom Cooperation

1. From Leadership Network study, *State of Church Planting USA*, available from www.leadnet.org.
2. Ibid.
3. Ibid.
4. The mission statement of Redeemer Presbyterian Church may be found on its Web site at www.redeemer.com.
5. The quotation in this paragraph comes from Warren Bird, "Church in the City," *Outreach* magazine (July–Aug. 2007).
6. Ibid.
7. Keller, Tim. *The Reason for God: Belief in an Age of Skepticism* (New York: Penguin, 2008).
8. Quotations in this paragraph come from a great resource: Tim Keller, "Why Plant Churches?" (February, 2002). Available from www.redeemer.com.
9. Appelton, Joanne. "Good to Great in Church Planting: Accelerating and Effectiveness in Church Planting"

(Leadership Network, May 2009). Available from www
.leadnet.org/papers.

6. Predictors of Success

1. From Leadership Network study, *State of Church Planting USA*, available from www.leadnet.org.
2. Ibid.
3. Ibid.
4. Ibid.
5. Ibid.
6. This section is adapted from Smith, Glenn, "Models for Raising Up Church Planters" (Leadership Network, Jan. 2007). Available from www.leadnet.org/churchplanting.
7. Church Planter's Training Program is available from CoachNet, www.coachnet.org.

7. Thriving

1. 2007 report for Center for Missional Research, North America Mission Board study. All churches in the study were connected with a denomination and had received funding in some way.
2. Ibid.
3. Ibid.
4. Ferguson, Dave, Jon Ferguson, and Eric Bramlett, *The Big Idea: Focus the Message, Multiply the Impact* (Grand Rapids, MI: Zondervan, 2007).
5. 2007 NAMB study.
6. Ibid.

8. House Churches

1. The surveys were conducted by the Barna Group, www.barna .org.

2. Center for Missional Research, North America Mission Board, Southern Baptist Convention.

3. Bird, Warren. "House Church Movement." In Charles Lippy, ed., *Encyclopedia of Religion in America* (Washington, DC: CQ Press, 2010).

4. Cole, Neil. *Organic Church: Growing Faith Where Life Happens* (San Francisco: Jossey-Bass, 2005); Cole, Neil. *Organic Leadership: Leading Naturally Right Where You Are* (Grand Rapids, MI: Baker, 2009); Cole, Neil. *Church 3.0: Upgrades for the Future of the Church* (San Francisco: Jossey-Bass, 2010).

5. This quotation comes from Towns, Elmer, Ed Stetzer, and Warren Bird. *Eleven Innovations in the Local Church: How Today's Leaders Can Learn, Discern, and Move into the Future* (Ventura, CA: Regal, June 2007): 25.

6. The quotation in this paragraph comes from Towns, Stetzer, Bird, *Eleven Innovations*, 25.

7. Ibid., 26.

8. Ibid., 27.

9. Barna, George. *Revolution* (Wheaton, IL: Tyndale, 2006).

9. Multisite Strategy

1. Based on unpublished Leadership Network research.

2. 2008 data; see Thumma, Scott, and Warren Bird. "Changes in American Megachurches" (Leadership Network, Sept. 2008): 8. Available from www.leadnet.org/megachurch.

3. Quotations taken from Vikki Broughton Hodges. "Community Church North to Open." *The Dispatch*, July 24, 2009. Available from www.the-dispatch.com/article/20090724/ARTICLES/ 907244012?Title=Community-Church-North-to-open.

4. Surratt, Geoff, Greg Ligon, and Warren Bird. *The Multi-Site Church Revolution: Being One Church in Many Locations* (Grand Rapids, MI: Zondervan, 2006); Surratt, Ligon, Bird. *A Multi-Site Church Roadtrip: Exploring the New Normal* (Grand Rapids, MI: Zondervan, 2006).

5. McConnell, Scott. *Multi-Site Churches: Guidance for the Movement's Next Generation* (Nashville, TN: B&H, 2009).
6. Material in this section adapted from Surratt, Geoff. "Should You Plant a Church or Launch a Campus?" Pastor's Toolbox, Dec. 24, 2008. Available from http://legacy.pastors.com/RWMT/default.asp?id=368&artid=11550&expand=1.
7. "Should Multisite Campuses Be Church Plants Instead?" *Christianity Today* (Oct. 2009): Vol. 53.
8. Ibid.

10. Rapid Growth

1. This research came from Stephen Gray and was reported in the study that Ed Stetzer conducted for Leadership Network. Gray then released many of his findings in a book, listed in our Bibliography: Gray, Stephen. *Planting Fast-Growing Churches* (Saint Charles, IL: ChurchSmart Resources, 2007).
2. Ibid.
3. Ibid.
4. Ibid.

11. Funding

1. From Leadership Network study, *State of Church Planting USA*, available from www.leadnet.org.
2. Unpublished survey of a thousand randomly selected Protestant churches across the United States conducted by LifeWay Research in November 2008.
3. From Leadership Network study, *State of Church Planting USA*, available from www.leadnet.org.
4. Ibid.

12. The New Scorecard

1. Quote from personal interview with Ed Stetzer.

2. This story from NorthWood is adapted and updated from Ed Stetzer, "Church Squared," July 3, 2007. Available from http://out reachmagazine.com/library/features/ja07ftrchurchsquared.asp.

3. Bruce, Deborah, and Cynthia Woolever. "U.S. Congregational Life Survey" (Louisville, KY: Presbyterian Church [U.S.A.] Research Services, 2002). For more information on the U.S. Congregational Life Survey, see www.uscongregations.org.

4. This section is adapted from a paper that Ed Stetzer and David Garrison wrote and distributed at the Exponential Conference April 20–23, 2009, Orlando, Florida. www.exponentialconfer-ence.org. It is not publicly available.

5. Niebuhr, Richard H. *Christ and Culture* (San Francisco: Harper and Row, 2001).

6. Miller, Donald. *Reinventing American Protestantism: Christianity in the New Millennium* (Los Angeles: University of California Press, 1997).

7. Hesselgrave, David. *Dynamic Religious Movements* (Kentwood, MI: Baker Book House, 1978).

13. Obstacles to Missional Replication

1. Maxwell, John C. *Developing the Leaders Around You: How to Help Others Reach Their Full Potential* (Nashville, TN: Nelson, 1995): 198.

2. Thumma, Scott, and Warren Bird. "Changes in American Megachurches" (Leadership Network, September 2008): 6. Available from www.leadnet.org/megachurch.

3. See Table 12.1 of this book.

4. Griffith, Jim, and Bill Easum. *Ten Most Common Mistakes Made by New Church Starts* (Duluth, GA: Chalice Press, 2008).

14. Conclusion

1. Bunyan, John. *The Holy War* (New Kensington, PA: Whitaker House, 1985).

2. Lewis, Robert, and Wayne Cordeiro, with Warren Bird. *Culture Shift: Transforming Your Church from the Inside Out* (San Francisco: Jossey-Bass, 2005): 91–92.
3. Cordeiro, Wayne. *Leading on Empty: Refilling Your Tank and Renewing Your Passion* (Grand Rapids, MI: Baker. 2009).
4. See also Scazzero, Pete, with Warren Bird. *The Emotionally Healthy Church: A Strategy for Discipleship That Actually Changes Lives*, Rev. ed. (Grand Rapids, MI: Zondervan, 2009).

ANNOTATED BIBLIOGRAPHY FOR CHURCH MULTIPLICATION

Addison, Steve. *Movements That Change the World*. Smyrna, DE: Missional Press, 2009.

> This book is for anyone who wants to follow Jesus and change the world. Movements that change the world are characterized by white-hot faith, commitment to a cause, contagious relationships, rapid mobilization, and adaptive methods. Jesus founded a missionary movement. His followers are called to continue his mission in the power of the Holy Spirit.

Allen, Roland. *Missionary Methods, St. Paul's or Ours?* Grand Rapids, MI: Eerdmans, 1962.

> Though not directly related to North American church planting, this is a seminal book in missiology. Allen posits that the key to evangelizing the world is the adoption of "Paul's strategy." Paul relied on trained lay leadership as pastors and elders. Allen's prescriptions can be applied to the North American scene with the development of lay church planting strategies. His focus on the Holy Spirit's role is also key to fostering church planting movements today.

Becker, Paul. *Dynamic Daughter Church Planting*. Vista, CA: Multiplication Ministries, 1996.

> This is the only book of its kind and is much needed. It provides church planting churches with the step-by-step guide that they need

to reproduce themselves. If you are planting a daughter church, you need this resource.

Brock, Charles. *Indigenous Church Planting*. Nashville: Broadman Press, 1981.

Brock's resources are time-tested and valuable. However, they do reflect a paradigm used more frequently in decades past. His ideas often come from his years of church planting in the Philippines among tribal people. As such, they will often relate well in a lower socioeconomic bracket in North America, but not to all contexts. The greatest value will be for indigenous lay persons seeking to plant churches in center cities or rural North America.

Browning, Dave. *Deliberate Simplicity: How the Church Does More by Doing Less*. Grand Rapids: Zondervan, 2009.

Pastor, church planter, and innovator Dave Browning wants to help churches structure themselves to reach an unlimited number of people in an unlimited number of places. He unpacks the six elements of a new equation for church development. These concepts—minimality, intentionality, reality, multility, velocity, and scalability—provide a realistic plan for streamlining church while maximizing impact.

Cole, Neil. *Church 3.0: Upgrades for the Future of the Church*. San Francisco: Jossey-Bass, 2010.

As a follow-up to *Organic Church*, this new book provides practical insight to encourage multiplication movements. He answers common questions and provides practical advice on everything from avoiding heresy to working with children. The book will provide challenges and insights to different kinds of churches, but it particularly focuses on those using organic, simple, and house church models.

Cole, Neil. *Organic Church: Growing Faith Where Life Happens*. San Francisco: Jossey-Bass, 2005.

According to international church starter and pastor Neil Cole, if we want to connect with young people and those who are not coming to church, we must go where people congregate. Cole shows readers how to plant the seeds of the kingdom of God in the places where life happens and where culture is formed—restaurants, bars, coffee-houses, parks, locker rooms, and neighborhoods. *Organic Church* offers a hands-on guide for demystifying this new model of church and shows the practical aspects of implementing it.

Comiskey, Joel. *Planting Churches That Reproduce*. Moreno Valley, CA: CCS, 2009.

> Planting a "church planting church" is often promised and rarely implemented for many in the world of church planting. In the search for a model that is culturally effective and highly reproducible, Comiskey has offered a levelheaded approach to house and cell church planting. His book offers a guide to the "root system" of a new church and how simplicity leads to high reproducibility. (Full disclosure: Ed wrote the foreword.)

Dale, Felicity. *Getting Started: A Practical Guide to House Church Planting*. Woodland Park, CO: Karis, 2003.

> There are many house church books out there (see a list at www .newchurches.com.) This one is unique in that it provides a clear and reproducible (dare I say "simple") method for planting churches that meet in homes. As Felicity describes it, anyone can do it, which is sort of her point!

Dale, Felicity, Tony Dale, and George Barna. *The Rabbit and the Elephant: Releasing the Mega Impact of Micro Churches*. Wheaton, IL: Tyndale, 2009.

> Much like a new litter of rabbits, the early church quickly grew and spread, and the world was transformed. By practicing "simple church"—whether we meet in office buildings, college dorm rooms, coffee shops, factories, or homes—the Holy Spirit expands these small gatherings to the far reaches of the globe.

Faircloth, Samuel D. *Church Planting for Reproduction*. Grand Rapids, MI: Baker Book House, 1991.

> Faircloth's book starts as a survey-oriented textbook, but quickly becomes a systematic church planting strategy. It is not geared toward North American planting, but this is not a shortcoming. This is one of the few principle-oriented books available that relate to North American planting. In this case, Faircloth calls his system PERT (a system of Program Evaluation and Review Technique). Regardless of the terminology, this is an important missiological resource for discerning North American planters.

Ferguson, Dave, and Jon Ferguson. *Exponential: How You and Your Friends Can Start a Missional Church Movement*. Grand Rapids, MI: Zondervan, 2010.

> Leaders of today's church have the ability to catalyze and contribute to a movement that will accomplish the mission of Jesus. *Exponential*

presents a Biblical strategy that explains how every Christ follower can successfully "reproduce" and maximize his or her impact for the kingdom of God.

Garrison, David. *Church Planting Movement: How God Is Redeeming a Lost World.* Richmond, VA: Wigtake Resources, 2003.

David Garrison's *Church Planting Movements* issues a challenge to traditional church planting strategy, not only through its exegesis of the Scriptural text, but through the distilled wisdom gained from case studies. Garrison makes a strong case for unpaid, local, lay leadership, planting rapidly reproducing small churches that exhibit characteristics of evangelism, prayer, and a persistent obedience to the Word of God.

Gray, Stephen. *Planting Fast-Growing Churches.* Saint Charles, IL: ChurchSmart Resources, 2007.

The authors surveyed 112 church plants and found some surprising data in the areas of leadership ability, financial support of the plant, conceptual freedom for the planter, coaching and training, core group, and ministries offered at the launch.

Halter, Hugh, and Matt Smay. *The Tangible Kingdom: Creating Incarnational Community.* San Francisco: Jossey-Bass, 2008.

Halter and Smay are real-life church leaders who record their lessons learned regarding the establishment of small missional communities of faith. The emphasis of the book is on the need for believers to leave the safe communal "bubble" we tend to establish for the real-world experience of God's kingdom arriving among the culture. With a strong focus toward ancient practices of faith regarding hospitality and friendship, this book can enhance a person's view of how the church interacts with their city on a pedestrian level.

Harrison, Rodney, Tom Cheyney, and Don Overstreet. *Spin-Off Churches: How One Church Successfully Plants Another.* Nashville, TN: B&H Publishing Group, 2008.

The past two decades in Christendom have brought forth a proliferation of books about church planting. One denomination (Southern Baptist) has even set a goal to start fifty thousand new churches over the next twenty year period. *Spin-Off Churches* aims to serve as a solid resource that specifically defines how one established church can successfully sponsor or parent a new church into sustainable existence. (And, for full disclosure, Ed wrote the afterword in this book.)

Hirsch, Alan, and Darryn Altclass, *The Forgotten Ways Handbook: A Practical Guide for Developing Missional Churches*. Grand Rapids, MI: Baker, 2009.

This is a follow-up guide to Hirsch's popular 2007 title, *Forgotten Ways: Reactivating the Missional Church*, which talked about six elements of "Jesus movements" that come together to create hyperbolic growth through spontaneous expansion, a very similar idea to churches that multiply virally. The highly practical handbook shows how to implement the ideas of remembering what it means to be a transformative movement for Jesus. As the authors explain, "Our main purpose is to stir innovative missional action for Jesus"—something they believe any Christian can be part of.

Keller, Tim, and J. Allen Thompson. *Church Planting Manual*. New York: Redeemer Church Planting Center, 2002.

Keller and Thompson are two leading voices with great credibility. Thompson has written on church planting movements for years. Keller is helping to lead a movement of church planting and city transformation. This is an excellent resource. Rather than a standard text, it is a workbook, and thus has projects and assignments to work though. It also has an urban focus that is appropriate for their passion.

Logan, Robert E. *Be Fruitful and Multiply*. Saint Charles, IL: ChurchSmart Resources, 2006.

Ed wrote the foreword to this book and here's an excerpt: "There is little that is done in North American church planting leadership that was not developed or influenced by Bob Logan. Few realize that before his keen insights and organizational acumen, church planters did not go through assessment, boot camps, and coaching networks. Why did Bob do these things? Because he cares about church planting and church planters. For thirty years we have taken baby steps toward true biblical church planting—but books like these will help us break through to movements."

Mannoia, Kevin. *Church Planting: The Next Generation*. Indianapolis, IN: Light and Life Communication, 1994.

Mannoia focuses on systems. He describes the system of his Free Methodist denomination which mirrors that used by many others, especially the one created by Bob Logan. Mannoia divides the system into the following categories: Parent Church Network, Profile Assessment System, New Church Incubator, Recruitment Network, Pastor Factory, Church Planter's Summit, Maturing Church Cluster, Strategic Planning Network, Harvest 1000, and the Meta-Church

Network. This will be a particularly helpful resource for groups and denominations that do not have a church planting system.

Moore, Ralph. *How to Multiply Your Church: The Most Effective Way to Grow God's Kingdom.* Ventura, CA: Regal, 2009.

Existing congregations simply cannot add enough believers to keep up with the population growth around them. The good news is that by multiplying—that is, by steadily and strategically planting new churches that, in turn, plant new churches—the global Church can create more of what Ralph Moore calls "harvest points." (Again, for full disclosure, Ed wrote the foreword to this book.)

Nevius, John L. *Planting and Development of Missionary Churches.* Nutley, NJ: Presbyterian and Reformed Publishing Company, 1958.

Nevius is not well known in North American church planting for good reason. His influence is primarily found in Korea. However, his ideas influence North American planting. His emphasis on indigenous ministry (three-selfs) helped spark the remarkable growth of the Korean church.

Patterson, George, and Richard Scoggins. *Church Multiplication Guide.* Pasadena, CA: William Carey Library, 2003.

This book is very practical in addressing the areas of church multiplication and reproduction from ten points of view in response to Jesus' command.

Ridley, Charles R. *How to Select Church Planters.* Pasadena, CA: Charles E. Fuller Evangelistic Association, 1988.

Ridley's writing and training have become the standard used in North America to evaluate potential church planters. This book, though difficult to find, is the standard text and should be required reading for everyone who selects church planters.

Roberts, Bob, Jr. *The Multiplying Church: The New Math for Starting New Churches.* Grand Rapids, MI: Zondervan, 2008.

Bob Roberts asks this question of the Western world: why are we not seeing the rapid expansion of church planting here as is evident in other parts of the world? With his normal wit and excitement about God's kingdom, Roberts unearths the principles of church planting from the early church. Presenting the principles in clear fashion, these lessons and exhortations from a seasoned veteran will benefit both the novice and experienced church planter. (Full disclosure: Ed wrote the foreword.)

Steffan, Tom. *Passing the Baton: Church Planting That Empowers*. La Habra, CA: Center for Organizational & Ministry Development, 1997.

This book can fool you. It is "about" international church planting, but it is very applicable to U.S. planting, particularly in the inner city. (Steffan does training for World Impact, a pacesetter in planting indigenous churches among the urban poor.) His emphasis on empowerment is an important addition to the training of every urban church planter.

Stevenson, Phil. *The Ripple Church: Multiply Your Ministry by Parenting New Churches*. Indianapolis, IN: Wesleyan, 2004.

There are few books that are focused on "churches planting churches." Phil has provided a tool to help churches get involved—it is an advocacy book with many helpful tools. It won't tell you how to plant, but it will help you gather some partner churches on the journey.

Tidsworth, Floyd, Jr. *Life Cycle of a New Congregation*. Nashville, TN: Broadman, 1992.

The title is misleading as the text deals little with the actual life cycle. Instead, it primarily focuses on the birth of a new church and then its reproduction—with little about the life cycle in the middle. Tidsworth is former director of the Southern Baptist's Home Mission Board's church planting department.

Timmis, Stephen (ed.). *Multiplying Churches: Reaching Communities Through Church Planting*. Hearn, Ross-shire, UK: Christian Focus Publications, 2000.

This book is an advocacy book, rather than a "how-to." The authors are quite clear about their intent: "What the book is trying to do is to move church planting up the church agenda, and focus upon the principles rather than the practice." I believe they accomplished the former but I am not sure about the latter. Their book is strong on encouraging people toward church planting but it is really too small (128 pages) to address the principles. The chapter on ecclesiology is excellent, as is the closing chapter.

Towns, Elmer L., and Douglas Porter. *Churches That Multiply*. Kansas City: Beacon Hill Press, 2003.

This book is a little different from many others listed and that may be its strength. It is a series of Bible studies written in the down-to-earth style of Elmer Towns. It is not a "how-to" book; rather, it is a series of Bible studies geared toward lay people in the church. The working prepublication title was *Our Church Planting a Church*, which describes the book well.

This list is much shorter than the list in Ed's earlier book, *Planting Missional Churches*. Here we wanted to highlight only the books that focus on or have application to church multiplication movements. Many excellent books exist about other aspects of church planting (including, we might add, our own earlier books).

THE AUTHORS

Ed Stetzer has planted several churches and has trained pastors and church planters on five continents. He holds two master's degrees and two earned doctorates, and has written dozens of articles and books. Ed is a contributing editor for *Christianity Today*, a columnist for *Outreach* magazine and *Catalyst Monthly*, serves on the advisory council of *Sermon Central* and *Christianity Today*'s Building Church Leaders, and is frequently cited or interviewed in news outlets such as USA Today and CNN.

Ed is visiting professor of Research and Missiology at Trinity Evangelical Divinity School, visiting research professor at Southeastern Baptist Theological Seminary, and has taught at fifteen other colleges and seminaries. He also serves on the Church Services Team at the International Mission Board of the Southern Baptist Convention.

Ed's primary role is as president of LifeWay Research and LifeWay's missiologist-in-residence, based in Nashville, Tennessee.

Warren Bird was part of a church plant in his childhood (fifteen years). After seminary he planted one church (four years), served on pastoral staff of another church plant (eleven years), and served as a volunteer leader in two other church plants (one year and two years).

Among the twenty-one books he has coauthored, one tells the story of a dozen church planters, *Starting a New Church* (book-with-DVD, Beacon Hill Press, Kansas City, 2003), and three others are coauthored for pastors who are church planters: *Emotionally Healthy Church* (Pete Scazzero, New Life, Queens, New York), *Culture Shift* (Wayne Cordeiro, New Hope, Honolulu, Hawaii), and *Multi-Site Church Revolution* (Geoff Surratt, Seacoast Church, Mt. Pleasant, South Carolina).

Warren currently directs the research division at Leadership Network, a Dallas-based nonprofit that helps innovative Christian leaders increase their impact. This role includes several types of research with church planters.

Warren has also served as an adjunct professor at Alliance Theological Seminary for thirteen years. He has received academic degrees from Wheaton College (B.A., M.A.), Alliance Theological Seminary (M.Div.), and Fordham University (Ph.D.).

Ed Stetzer has written the following books:

Planting New Churches in a Postmodern Age (2003)
Perimeters of Light: Biblical Boundaries for the Emerging Church (with Elmer Towns, 2004)
Breaking the Missional Code (with David Putman, 2006)
Planting Missional Churches (2006)
Comeback Churches (with Mike Dodson, 2007)
11 Innovations in the Local Church (with Elmer Towns and Warren Bird, 2007)
Compelled by Love: The Most Excellent Way to Missional Living (with Philip Nation, 2008)
Lost and Found: The Younger Unchurched and Churches that Reach Them (with Richie Stanley and Jason Hayes, 2009)

Warren Bird has coauthored twenty-one books, including

The Emotionally Healthy Church: A Strategy for Discipleship That Actually Changes Lives, Pete Scazzero with Warren Bird, (2003) (Received Gold Medallion award)